Also by Hubert Bromma

HOW TO INVEST IN REAL ESTATE AND PAY LITTLE OR NO TAXES

HOW TO INVEST IN REAL ESTATE WITH YOUR IRA AND 401(K) AND PAY LITTLE OR NO TAXES

Related Titles from McGraw-Hill

BUILDING REAL ESTATE WEALTH IN A CHANGING MARKET
by John Schaub

RENT TO OWN by Robert Irwin

BUY, RENT, AND SELL by Robert Irwin

How to Invest in Offshore Real Estate and Pay Little or No Taxes

How to Invest in Offshore Real Estate and Pay Little or No Taxes

Hubert Bromma

New York   Chicago   San Francisco   Lisbon   London
Madrid   Mexico City   Milan   New Delhi   San Juan
Seoul   Singapore   Sydney   Toronto

The *McGraw·Hill* Companies

Copyright © 2008 by Hubert Bromma. All rights reserved. Printed in the United States of America. Except as permitted under the United States Copyright Act of 1976, no part of this publication may be reproduced or distributed in any form or by any means, or stored in a database or retrieval system, without prior written permission of the publisher.

1 2 3 4 5 6 7 8 9   FGR/FGR   0 9 8 7

ISBN-13: 978-0-07-147009-4
ISBN-10: 0-07-147009-3

This publication is designed to provide accurate and authoritative information in regard to the subject matter covered. It is sold with the understanding that neither the author nor the publisher is engaged in rendering legal, accounting, or other professional service. If legal advice or other expert assistance is required, the services of a competent professional person should be sought.

—From a Declaration of Principles jointly adopted by Committee of the American Bar Association and a Committee of Publishers.

McGraw-Hill books are available at special discounts to use as premiums and sales promotions, or for use in corporate training programs. For more information, please write to the Director of Special Sales, Professional Publishing, McGraw-Hill, Two Penn Plaza, New York, NY 10121-2298. Or contact your local bookstore.

Contents

Acknowledgments

When I began my ventures into international real estate, I discovered that the process of making those investments involved considering many items—some that applied to all countries and others that were specific to the country or region that I was investigating. I have visited all of the countries in the examples included in this book and invested in several of them personally. I have also benefited from the firsthand experiences of those who made purchases. This book was written over an extensive period and involved many individuals who contributed to its results.

First, I would like to thank my most terrific supporter and fan, Lisa Bromma, who has been my constant travel companion and is always on the lookout for more and interesting material on global real estate investing. Lisa has spent many years as a real estate investor herself and is an author in her own right. Lisa is the best.

Mary Glenn of McGraw-Hill has been wonderful and extremely patient while I asked her to wait yet another month because of new world events!

Linda Fogel has been indispensable in all the books I have authored. She is the most experienced editor and proofreader, and without her capable and competent work, this book would not be in print.

In addition, my coworkers at The Entrust Group and International Bank and Trust have been invaluable. Irene Vann, Keith Stunek, Larry Sawyer, Haimanot Kassa, Nikki Edwards, Russ Anderson, Greg Freeman, and many others have been supporters and provided a lot of helpful information.

Finally, I want to thank my friends and professional acquaintances who have been supporters and resources for this book, including Brad Adderley, Dr. Markus Baldauf, Adriane Berg, Maggie Bird, Neal J. Block, T. Hale Boggs III, Diane Brewer, Derek Caldwell, Angie Coffee, Dr. Aldo Bruno Comploj, Ian Coulman, Jason Craig, Susan Diehl, Michael Dionne, Hadi Djamal, Peggy Engh, Joe Englert, Timothy Faries, Klaus Feurstein, Dr. Nico Francken, Robyn Goldy, Susan and Sidney Goodwill, Larry Grossman, Gottfried Halbmayr, Judith Hasenauer, Heino Helbock, Larry Heller, Richard Irvine, Moncia Jones, Vesna Jovanoska, Robert Kiyosaki, Harvey Labko, Richard Lipton, Albert K. W. Lo, Dorothe Mare, Natalie Marsan, Aleet Martin, Maura Ann McBreen, John McEwing, Anthony McKay, Anned Muse, Dr. Juan Pardini, David Pickering, Stefano Rampini, Anthony Riker, Udo Rothenbücher, Kurt Schubert, Jennifer Dizmang Smith, and Mary With. I would also like to thank the following organizations: Appleby Sperling and Kempe, Bermuda; Price Waterhouse Coopers, Bermuda; Bryan Cave, Santa Monica, California; Manatt Phelps and Phillips, Los Angeles; Butterfield and Butterfield; Bank of Bermuda; Baker McKenzie; Instant Access Properties, United Kingdom; The Pam Golding Group; Business Panama; the government of Panama; the Principality of Lichtenstein; and Lautze and Lautze.

Preface

You want to buy investment real estate abroad while getting tax breaks at the same time. It sounds like a great idea, and a lot of people are doing just that. Whether for romantic notions, sound investment strategies, retiring to your country of origin, or the fun of it, this book highlights the things that you should be aware of before diving into the world of global investing. But first, let's get this point out in front: Investing in real estate outside of the United States is not for the faint of heart. Not only do you have to be familiar with the tax laws in the United States—or work with professionals who are—you have to be aware of the laws, bureaucracies, and tax implications of the country you are investing in. It's even more risky if you are investing in a country whose government or economy isn't stable. Then there's the consideration of other languages, cultures, customs, and unfortunately, scams.

That said, there are many good reasons to venture beyond your backyard. You may be seeking a property for personal vacations and enjoyment, looking to retire in a less-expensive area, returning to your family's country, or desiring to expand your investment and income opportunities. If you feel comfortable making real estate investments in the United States, you have a good starting point. This book builds on your familiarity of purchasing real estate domestically and provides you with an overview of what's involved and the things you need to consider to venture further.

There are a number of things to consider as you forge ahead. Will you be living there? Will you be purchasing as an expatriate? How will you finance the purchase? Will you be using retirement funds? What are the tax consequences at home and abroad? What are the inheritance laws? These are just some of the things to ponder and evaluate before you take a leap into the global small investor real estate market. We will touch on all these aspects plus look at a sampling of real-life examples of investments in other countries. After you read this book, you will be able to begin your personal road to investing in real estate internationally. *How to Invest in Offshore Real Estate and Pay Little or No Taxes* is your fundamental guide on what to look out for, what your potential tax implications are, and how to avoid getting into trouble with the taxing authorities. I highly recommend that you explore and weigh all the factors before you delve into what could be an exciting and profitable investment—and adventure.

How to Invest in Offshore Real Estate and Pay Little or No Taxes

P A R T

Venturing Beyond
Your Own Backyard

If you look at websites and articles in journals and newspapers, you get the impression that investing in offshore real estate is a straight-forward process—as easy as buying something in your own back-yard. The pictures of beautiful income property on beaches and in mountains, deserts, and cities are tantalizing and are accompanied with enticing wording, such as "second home," "retirement opportunity," and "it will pay for itself." These properties market their appeal to investors, those who are or are considering expatriating, and soon-to-be retirees or the already retired. The big issues, such as location, exchange rates, taxes in the country of investment, the implications of taxes in one's own country, and what it really means to expatriate are not usually mentioned.

The first step is to pinpoint what's motivating you to consider investing offshore. Perhaps it's to fully retire or work less. Maybe your objective is to live in a temperate climate without concern for income when you reach age fifty. You also need to assess whether you have enough time to achieve your monetary goal within the terms of the lifestyle you wish to have. Being realistic is important. For instance, if you are forty-five, how many years do you have to find a way to live on a beach in a stable country with sufficient investments in a reliable market that gives you an income to live on when you are retired. Set your goals and objectives realistically. Balance your targets with your abilities and the abilities of those who you select to work with. If you go it alone, you will have to gain or already have a unique skill set.

Many of the basic things to consider before investing in other countries are similar to the the things you need to consider when investing in the United States—with an international twist. Having a worldview will help you make informed decisions and be successful in your investment choices. Understanding how politics and culture frame an economy, as well as how Americans are perceived, is valuable. The United States has a stable social, political, and economic system. It basically has a two-party system anchored by a constitution in which both parties wish to maintain a narrowly defined status quo. Change is not usually dramatic, and the population is generally satisfied. Even during severe economic problems, the country has survived and rebounded without a revolution or major change. However, the United States has not been as responsible as it could be in the environmental and international arena. After the cold war, the United States' emergence as the singular superpower as well as one of the largest consumers of the world's resources has led to some major difficulties around the globe, which have framed the perception that other countries have of the United States. It is essential to understand that the countries you are considering investing in may not share the same political, economic, and social goals that you are used to. This is not inherently bad or good; it's just different. Understanding the current situation as well as the history in countries you would like to invest in is essential in effectively meeting your long-term objective.

Here are some key areas that you should explore to help determine where you want to invest and whether this is what you want to do to meet your personal and financial goals. The book also includes a few personal accounts of people I have met. Although each chapter focuses on a particular country, the experiences and lessons learned could apply anywhere. I encourage you to read each chapter, even though you may not be interested in that particular country, to get a well-rounded view of what you may encounter. After considering all these points, in the end, you may like it just where you are. Investing outside of your backyard can take more effort, but it can also be an exciting and rewarding adventure. It all depends on your objectives and the goals you set to get there.

Price vs. Cost

Price in itself does not determine the value of an investment property. When purchasing a property, you look at whether it's in concert with your goals, and other factors such as appreciation and cash flow. And then there's the actual cost of the acquisition, which is important to take into account. Price is what first attracts you to the deal—and it is negotiable. But almost without exception throughout the world, the agreed-on price does not include the costs to complete the purchase. In the United States, you can easily calculate the costs because they are generally consistent with a HUD-1 closing statement. Outside the United States, the costs vary from country to country. Many of the elements are similar, so you can translate the knowledge you've gained from U.S. transactions, but some you may not have any experience with. For example, in France, the fee level can be affected by the age of the property—new properties have lower fees. Some countries have stamp duties, value-added taxes, and a variety of registration and conveyance fees. In addition, when you are investing beyond your backyard, double taxation, currency rates, and international mortgage rates can make the purchase more expensive than anticipated.

Tax (Dis)Advantages

Investing outside of the United States adds another tax dimension, so it's a good idea to understand the tax codes of the country that you are investing in. When determining whether an investment property will generate positive cash flow, you must include the tax implications of the income in your calculation, because U.S. taxpayers are taxed on their worldwide income. You should also take into account that there are certain legal tax advantages available in the United States when investing in property. For example, you can acquire investment property with your retirement funds, which offers tax-free or tax-deferred opportunities, or you can make tax-deferred 1031 exchanges of like-kind property. Some of these tax advantages are not available outside the United States. You cannot do a 1031 exchange for property outside the United States. You can, however, invest self-directed Individual Retirement Accounts (IRAs) and 401(k) money everywhere, but you may still be obligated to pay taxes in another country. For instance, with a Roth IRA, you pay tax once and then any profits made are tax free—tax free forever in the United States, that is. It does not mean they are tax free outside of the United States. No country outside the United States recognizes American retirement plans and so local taxes may apply.

Growth of Your Investment—As Solid as the Ground You Walk On

Historically, real estate has appreciated at a better rate than other investments. Stocks may come and go, but most real estate will always be there. Furthermore, not much new real estate is being produced, and the demand is high. But just like picking stocks, identifying real estate has to be done with knowledge and careful research, whether by you or your advisors. Look into eminent domain laws—can the government easily preempt your property and for what reasons? Are there environmental concerns that may affect your investment? Will that beach be there in twenty years or will a shortage of resources change the desirability of the area? What sort of zoning laws exist? What will happen to your investment if the area is overdeveloped?

Property usually appreciates in value as demand increases. Look at the appreciation of the location in constant currency value over time. Measure time in decades for a better view. You may be interested in having your property generate income, unless your investment strategy is based solely on appreciation. Having both is ideal—holding for long-term appreciation and positive cash flow is like having a strong stock that pays dividends. Rental income can have tax benefits and provide leverage for other investments.

The old saw of "location, location, location" is international. Before exploring property outside the United States, it is a good idea to understand locations here and their ability to generate income and provide appreciation. You may discover that it makes more sense to invest in your own backyard, but if you do decide to go offshore, you will know what to compare and contrast to make a good investment.

Emotional Considerations

Your investment choice may be an emotionally wise one but not a financially wise one. What is your goal? To satisfy a longing to have an apartment in Paris or beachfront property on a warm island? Because it's there and because you want it can confuse and confound great decisions that you are capable of making. If you really want a beach home or a mountain chalet or a home among the vines, that becomes your objective. All you have to do is make the money to meet and sustain that objective. If the purpose is investment income from cash flow or appreciation, leave emotions out of your decision making. Sometimes this is hard, but the true investor does not buy based on emotion alone. Use emotion wisely. However, don't discount what your goal may be. If what you really want is to retire to a beachfront house in the Caribbean, then don't settle for an affordable apartment in a city. However, if your goal is to subsidize your income, it might not matter where the property is located.

When Thinking Globally, Act Locally

Evaluate where you want to buy in terms of the "local" perspective. Around the world, people perceive nationality, institutions, leadership, government, economic stability, international debt or surplus, ethnicity, geography, environmental practices, religion, and laws in many different ways. As an American, you may perceive another nationality based on what you read in the news, a local restaurant that supposedly represents that country's cuisine, immigrants that you've met, or prejudices that you have based on stereotypes. When you visit the country, the perceptions and stereotypes that you have developed may cloud your ability to see things as they are. If you are looking for investment opportunities, it's best to come with an open mind. If you don't know the language and the culture, you may be very surprised by how the general population treats you if you are on a fact-finding mission. You may find that individuals and professionals that you meet have opinions about your nationality and culture. If you have a clear vision of what you want to know grounded in a plan that you have developed, and you have done some research before you arrive, you are more likely to have success and not be traveling seventeen hours just for a nice time (although that is always a part of your real estate investment journey).

Political and Economic Risks

When investing overseas, evaluate whether the country has a stable political system. Some countries that we label as unstable because of political perceptions can be quite stable and vice versa. For example, most Americans perceive Cuba as unstable, which is actually not the case. It has had the same leader since 1958. The country underwent some internal change after it lost its benefactor, the former Soviet Union, but the extent of change to the power elite was minimal.

Panama, a popular country to invest in, is now a client state of the United States. The hegemony over Panama makes the country stable de facto, although events can change based on the government's foreign policy. The use of Panama for money laundering by other countries and their citizens, for example, could change the stability of the country and even the region. Fortunately, Panama is not interested in becoming a country widely known for illicit activities. Europe as a whole has been stable since the end of World War II until 1989, when the Soviet Union imploded, and the countries affected suddenly found that they could self-determine their future. Today, Europe consists of solid independent states. If you choose to buy real estate in Europe, it is unlikely to be appropriated from you without some semblance of due process. This is as stable as you can get.

One thing to remember: If a country is a client state of a large power, such as the United States, it does not make it inherently politically stable. Some of those countries are in transition, and the investment climate may be tentative. Be aware of what is happening politically, inside and outside the country, and the role the country or region plays in the global picture.

It's easy to comprehend how a country that is politically risky or steeped in violence can dramatically affect real property investment decisions, but don't overlook political decisions made by stable countries that could affect your property investments. In the coming decade, the recognition of global warming may affect policies in different countries as they look at the generation of emissions and mitigating their effect on the planet. If you are looking at long-term investments, evaluations of this kind are essential.

It is also important to have a macro view regarding the economic system of your real estate investment. Ask yourself how the economic system plays into political decisions, which could influence the attitude toward property ownership or the value of the currency. For example, the United States' economic system emanated from land and property ownership, and its political system and laws revolve around that. You want to invest in a country in which the government has minimized the warlike tendencies to have your real and personal property appropriated so that your interest will be protected. The effect of war on- and offshore could have a dramatic effect over time on your investment property. It could be gone, except the dirt, or someone could have legally appropriated it without your knowledge.

Sometimes, governments appropriate property for what is perceived to be, and many times is, for the common good. Some governments are arbitrary, and some act on caprice to modify your ability to transact your real property and business interest. It is not unusual to have governments appropriate property by making it economically disadvantageous for you to own the property. Even the property you bought in one political climate may be subject to different laws after the next election. Investment in official kleptocracies is strongly not recommended. Does the country have enormous public debt but fails to do anything about it? It can happen in any stable government. Not only will your currency be affected, but also the pressure on the government's future needs can affect your investment. If you are using U.S. dollars for your investment, look into how strong it is relative to other currencies. If the dollar is worth 25 percent less from one year to the next, your investment decision may change. If you have already invested when the dollar bought more, you are hopefully pleased.

Shifting Sands and Winds

As the global population increases, from an investor's perspective this can mean that land and resources are dear, and demand will remain high. However, this can also cause governments to dramatically shift their priorities. The change in global ecological conditions may prompt a different use of a property, such as for wind farms, nuclear power, water resources, or reclamation. For example, China has appropriated large tracts of land for the public good without just compensation to feed its need for hydroelectric power. Even in the United States, eminent domain has often been used for social good without adequate just compensation being paid to the landowner. But as long as there are societies and countries that feel that population expansion will be to the benefit of the globe's resources, the demand for property will continue. You may get really good investment deals in countries that have population expansion and appear to be powerhouses in the making. But what if the country chooses to overexpand, changing that lovely remote area into overcrowded high-rises. Also consider that the property you buy may be affected by natural events: earthquakes, tsunamis, typhoons, avalanches. Of course, these could happen in the United States, but do you know how the country you are considering handles such disasters? Do they have adequate building codes, preventive measures, national insurance, and aid? Also important to consider are changes that may take years to unfold. One of the major topics today is world climate change, which is unquestionably a major factor in deciding where you might invest. Global warming is not a new topic; many saw this coming in the early 1960s when they witnessed the glaciers in Switzerland and Canada, among other places, recede. So keep your eyes and ears open for what is happening around you. In the process, you may find that the agenda of an attractive website might not meld with yours.

When in Rome . . .

To make your real estate investment opportunities fare well in other countries and societies, consider the following.

Learn the language. Having just a small vocabulary goes a long way in the success of your investment. Knowing past, present, and future tense is very helpful. After all, that is the time line in which your real estate deal operates.

Learn the culture and local customs. Read up on and experience the culture. The culture you see on vacation is different from day to day. Religion makes up a large portion of culture and society. Whether it is nonexistent, polytheistic, monotheistic, all have an influence on the society in which you plan to do business. Failure to understand and respect the nuances and roles that culture, customs, and religion play can cause your deal to fall apart or change adversely. Knowledge and understanding is power. Humility on your part is not weakness.

Understand the local economy. The local economy is usually different from the national economy. What makes the local economy self-sustaining: building aircraft, growing wine, services and to whom, education, fishing, tourism, a combination thereof? How does this fit into your personal and real estate goals and objectives, in both the short and long term? Is the local economy working, and what is its future? Will the area be deserted or abandoned in a few years? All these factors can affect your investment.

Find local professionals that you can trust. Unless you are intending to live in the country in which you are investing, it's likely that you won't be able to be there for the entire transaction, not to mention when unexpected problems come up. This is where it helps to find local representation. For instance, in Spain, the completion of a mortgage must take place in front of an appointed notary with all parties involved in the purchase, including the seller, the lawyers, the buyer, and lender. If you can't be there because of other obligations or simply distance, you can assign power of attorney to a local agent who can sign on your behalf. Hiring a local property manager or letting agent who is qualified to work with international clients could keep things going smoothly. A local property manager would be familiar with the way things are done in the area and know which tradespeople to contact if something needs to be repaired. Having someone local find tenants, prepare rental agreements, deal with utility bills, collect rents, and visit the property on a regular basis is a must.

Is It Worth It?

With so much to take into account, you may wonder whether it's even worth the trouble. The answer to that depends on your personal circumstances: what your goals are, how much you can afford, and how comfortable you are in dealing with new situations. There are a wide range of investment opportunities, from the ridiculously expensive to the amazingly affordable. Despite the additional challenges that international real estate investment may pose, it can be an excellent investment. Diversifying your portfolio by buying property in different countries can help cushion you against economic downturns in a particular area. Or you may find that you can enter the market easier in a less expensive country, giving you the opportunity to leverage these investments over time. Then, of course, there's always the good fortune of snapping up something in an up-and-coming country. Investing in a real asset as compared with an intangible one, such as a stock, can provide more stability. Property tends to hold its value better than other commodities, and historically it has provided a good return on investment. Or, having an investment portfolio may not be your goal—you may just want a nice, less expensive place to retire to. Regardless of your reasons or circumstances, once you're ready to buy something, the first thing you need is money. So let's take a look at some of the money matters to consider when buying offshore.

Money Makes the World Go 'Round

When you are ready to purchase a property, it's time to open a local bank account and, if needed, explore options for obtaining a mortgage. Currency exchange rates must be taken into account when purchasing and maintaining a property. Avoid surprises and check the fees, commissions, wire charges, and exchange rates when you establish an account. Also look into what your current bank charges. To avoid multiple fees and commissions, transfer as much as possible if the exchange rate is at a favorable moment. There are no regulations governing the exchange rates that a bank can use, so be prepared for the bank to give you a rate that provides it some profit, which usually means that you will not receive the "published" rate. Banks aren't the only way to exchange money however. Check with the local people assisting you with your purchase for information on alternate means that may have lower fees and a better exchange rate.

Timing Is Everything

With exchange rates, one day can make a difference, so know when the funds will be transferred and when they are to arrive. Verify the receiving bank's rate of exchange and how many days it takes the bank to handle the transfer. Calculate this into your purchase price. One of our clients learned the hard way. Tom was ready to purchase his pied-à-terre in Paris, so he transferred funds directly from the United States to the escrow account at the bank in France. He calculated the exchange rate on the Internet on the day of transfer and expected to receive €425,000 (euros) to pay for the apartment. At the closing, he discovered that he had only €414,000. Tom protested that someone had shorted him on the exchange rate. Unfortunately, here is what happened.

Tom transferred the money on a day that the exchange was indeed favorable—if the exchange had taken place on that day. The money was sent from his U.S. bank on the day he requested, but the French bank didn't receive the funds until two days later. And then the bank did not exchange the money until four days later, when the rates went against Tom. The funds were actually credited to the bank on the date it received the dollars, but it disintermediated the exchange to profit from the lower rate.

Tom complained to the *notaire* (legal agent) who was helping him with the transaction, but there wasn't anything to be done. The bank had chosen when it wanted to exchange the money, and Tom was out €11,000. The notaire would not, of course, close the deal unless another €11,000 was forthcoming. Then Tom also discovered that there were wiring fees and conversion fees that totaled another $30 from his U.S. bank and €25 from the French bank. But at least these were small surprises in comparison to the €11,000 exchange difference.

Favored Currencies

If the country you are purchasing in desires your currency, you may get a better exchange rate. You may even be able to negotiate the rate and fees, obtaining more for your dollar. When I was twelve years old, I became one of the first foreign currency day traders in the mid-1950s in West Germany. My mother gave me 50 pfennig a day to use as I wished, which in those days was a lot of money and would buy me an entry to the newsreels. But I had nothing left over for my favorite crumble cake, which cost 5 pfennig. So to have both, I would have to find the difference on the sidewalk or find a way to make a quick 10 percent on my 50 pfennig. Every school day I would wait for the bus at the main train station in Munich, which had two currency exchanges: an American one and a German one. The exchange rate was about 3 percent different for U.S. dollars, or in my case, I was just dealing with pennies. I saved two days of my allowance and took my one German mark (100 pfennigs) to the American exchange and got 28 cents. Then I went to the German exchange and traded for 105 pfennigs, and now you get the idea. It took about five minutes to go from one exchange to the other, and shortly I had enough for two days of crumble cake and newsreels! I didn't do this every day because the novelty would wear off between the American and German exchanges for the amount of money involved.

There was a time in Italy when the U.S. dollar was considered a favorable currency. Italians were busy offering to buy dollars at very good prices. The banks in Italy would give you 1,600 lire for the dollar. The exchange offices would give you 1,500 lire, and some discount individuals would give you 1,700. There were black markets where you could get even more. Prices would be bid up, and even banks would outbuy each other. But when it came to selling lire, the rates were a lot different. Because dollars were dear and lire were not, you would get one dollar for every 2,000 lire. Today, Italy uses the euro, which is considered a favorable currency. At one time, 88 U.S. cents got you one euro. In 2006, it went up to $1.30 for one euro. That means the price of European goods is significantly higher for American consumers and that American goods are significantly cheaper for those with euros.

The moral of these stories is that you need to become grounded in currency exchange rates, how money moves, and international economics. Knowing when to hold onto the currency you have in the country of investment and when to send money to another place is advantageous. You also need to know who your bankers and exchangers are, and they may not always be the same depending on the situation, the country, or the currency you are working with. With a good understanding of currencies and exchanges, you can make beneficial offshore investments in real estate. You can have your crumble cake and eat it too.

What Am I Getting for My Money?

When dealing with real estate, it's important to have a fundamental understanding of why some properties hold their value and others don't. Many people ask whether real estate is more expensive now compared with yesterday. Unfortunately, there's no clear answer, because it depends on so many factors. Economies change, laws change, people and populations change, demand and supply change, and politics and the environment change—all affect how people perceive real estate. In most areas, the demand changes depending on all of these factors. In some areas, such as the Hamptons, Beverly Hills, the French Riviera, and Marbella, the demand and supply remain fairly static. All of these are desirable communities in different parts of the world. They are in stable countries that have relatively stable governments. Compare these places with Beirut, Havana, Malaysia, Sri Lanka. These are desirable areas as well, but the political issues concerning these areas make investment real estate more difficult.

When investing in real estate, it's important to take a long view to see how economies and trends play out. For instance, fifty years ago, the German economy was in the midst of recovering after World War II. The exchange rate was then four marks to the dollar. To Americans, the exchange rate made property in West Germany appear to be very inexpensive compared to similarly priced properties in the United States. During the same time, the United States was experiencing an expansion of the real estate market. Recognizing that a large factor in the price of property was the exchange rate resulted in shrewd Americans buying real property in West Germany for investment purposes. And an added advantage was that Germany was successfully rebuilding its economy with generous Marshall Plan funds and new investment opportunities. To give you an example, let's compare a property in Germany and one in California over a fifty-year span of time.

In 1956, the property in Germany sold for the equivalent of $18,000. In 2006, it sold for $3.2 million. Located in the state of Bavaria in the southern part of Germany, here's what you got:

Lakefront property, three acres; main house has two stories, with three bedrooms, one bath, living room, dining area, and kitchen. The guest house has two rooms and a garage. Thirty miles south of Munich.

The property in California, which sold for $18,000 in 1956, sold for $1.1 million in 2006.

Architect-designed one-story home, with four bedrooms, two baths, living room, dining room, family room, eat-in kitchen, and garage. A third of an acre in a secluded community fifteen miles north of San Francisco.

In these two examples, the following issues come into play. You have a war-torn country that was in the midst of economic recovery, and a state that was in the midst of prosperous growth located in a country that suffered little damage during the war. Both areas remained desirable and continued to prosper. Which investment would you have chosen? Where you buy, when you buy, and what you buy is the same everywhere. But when you are investing abroad, you have to add the exchange rate.

An investment in a war-torn, unstable country where investments are inexpensive and the dollar is strong may pay huge dividends some time in the future when the country stabilizes and rebounds. This is occurring in some countries in South America. But some countries are in areas where recovery is always in question because they are in the crossroads of competing interests or conflicting religious differences or have desirable natural resources. These factors must always be in the forefront when considering your investments.

International Mortgages

If you do not have ready cash to pay for your investment, you need to borrow money. Depending on the country and type of investment, there are several options.

Local bank. Taking a mortgage in a bank located in your country of investment may be constrained by currency exchange control rules. Another concern is that local banks or lending institutions may charge nonresidents higher rates of interest.

Bank where you are a resident. You may have trouble finding a bank that is willing to loan you money for an investment outside the country. In addition, if you are using retirement funds, you may have other considerations (see Chapter 4, "Using IRAs Offshore").

Developer. New developments sometimes offer their own mortgages and financing to increase sales.

International institution. There are a growing number of international mortgage brokers that offer products that are tailored to meet the needs of international investors. These are good options, because these companies are familiar with the processes and issues applicable to nonresident investments, which a local bank may not be fully aware of.

So now that you know about the options for paying for the property, let's look at the tax implications.

Death and Taxes

For some investors, tax—or the avoidance thereof—is the driving force behind going offshore, but for the great majority of well-off individuals considering offshore investment, tax is not the primary issue. These investors reside in high-tax areas, such as countries in the European Union, the United States, Canada, and Japan, and they pay their taxes. Their motivation in purchasing real estate in other countries is to get higher returns, without any intention to evade taxes in their home countries. These investors often look at countries that are more lightly regulated or have huge growth potential.

Although tax shouldn't be the most important consideration when choosing a property, it's not to be overlooked. The tax implications vary in complexity and impact according to the country you are investing in and what you intend to do with the property. In addition, you need to take into account that the United States taxes you on your worldwide income. Taxes levied on international property investments usually fall into the following categories:

- Capital acquisitions tax, inheritance tax, stamp duty, or transfer tax for purchasing, inheriting, or transferring property
- Local and national property taxes and land tax for owning and/or residing on the property
- Income tax on rents received, of which there may be additional taxes imposed on nonresident or foreign landlords

- Capital gains tax, gift taxes, or death duties and estate taxes for disposing of the property

To avoid or minimize taxation, there are countries or jurisdictions with no taxes on income or capital gains, such as the Turks and Caicos Islands. However, some of these tax havens are an option only for the very wealthy who are willing to contribute substantially to the local economy and purchase luxury real estate, and some of these locations limit the number of foreigners permitted residence or work permits. In comparison, governments in nontax-haven countries tend to impose fewer restrictions on nonresidents purchasing property, yet the likelihood is that you will face more taxes on your investment. But some high-tax countries provide advantages over the long term. For instance, in France rents over the last fifty years have averaged a net operating income (NOI) of about 7 percent, which is not terrific. But if you hold onto the property for at least fifteen years, your tax on capital gains is vastly reduced. And when you consider that property values have gone up about the same rate as rents, you will have an enormous gain.

To lessen or bypass taxes, some property investors choose to purchase international property via an offshore company or trust, often established in a low-tax jurisdiction. Trusts in particular can be effective in protecting investors and their beneficiaries from high estate and death taxation. Some countries have no provisions in their tax regulations to tax the underlying assets of a foreign company, so an offshore company can be a tax-efficient vehicle to hold property investments.

Expatriating: A Permanent Option

If you are a U.S. resident or citizen, one way to reduce taxes is to permanently give up your citizenship and residency. Before choosing this route, you need to fully grasp the implications: The United States frowns on those expatriating for tax purposes by making it nearly impossible to return to the United States. This law has been largely unenforced, but it exists nevertheless. In addition, you are still liable for tax for ten years after expatriating on all income originating from the United States if you give up your residence or citizenship for tax reasons. If you're thinking that you could just state that you did not expatriate for tax reasons, it's not that easy. Tax reasons simply apply if you had a net worth of $2 million or more since 2004, or if your average annual tax over three years was $124,000 beginning in 2004. The amounts are indexed for inflation for years starting in 2004 and thereafter. By expatriating, however, your future income earned outside the United States will not be subject to U.S. taxes. How much of an advantage that equals is for you to decide. And regardless of your net worth or your average taxes, you still have some tax reporting to do after expatriation.

In actuality, few people choose to give up their U.S. residency or citizenship, and those who do, do so for nontax reasons, such as returning to their country of birth or family ancestry. If you do choose to give up your U.S. citizenship or residence status, make sure that you have first made arrangements to acquire citizenship elsewhere and obtain a passport. And, if possible, get a passport from a country that bases its income tax system on residence rather than citizenship. For U.S. citizens, Canada is one of the more attractive countries for an alternate citizenship.

Avoiding Double Taxation

Because the United States taxes you on your worldwide income, you may be double taxed. If you are living and working outside the United States, you can take advantage of the foreign earned income exclusion, which exempts a certain amount of your offshore earned income from U.S. income tax. In addition, if your employer is a foreign person, you do not have to pay supplementary taxes like Social Security or Medicare. To take advantage of this exclusion, you must reside outside the United States for at least 330 days in any twelve-consecutive-month period. The United States also has tax treaties with some countries that permit you to receive credit for taxes you may have to pay in the United States and also in the country of investment.

In countries that have high tax rates on earned income, the foreign tax credit may be a better option than the exclusion of foreign earned income. For example, France imposes a tax rate of 45 percent on your earnings, but in the United States, the tax rate is 33 percent. So if you earn $100,000, the tax is $45,000 in France but only $33,000 in the United States. You can thus offset your U.S. tax 100 percent by $33,000 of the tax paid to France, with your total taxes then being $45,000. If you choose to use the foreign earned income exclusion, which was $82,400 in 2006, with an income of $100,000, you would pay U.S. taxes on the remaining $17,600. The French tax that you would pay on the amount that is excluded from U.S. tax cannot be used as a tax credit in the United States, but you would still get a credit for the foreign taxes paid on the $17,600 remaining. Basically, you could still end up paying $45,000 to France and zero taxes to the United States, but other combinations of tax rates between the two countries could produce different results. Generally, if the U.S. tax rates are higher, the foreign earned income exclusion is better than the foreign tax credit.

The U.S. foreign tax credit is not limited to taxes on earned income. As a foreign investor, you may be subject to income taxes, real estate gains, or other capital gains. You can claim a credit to offset your U.S. taxes for the taxes paid to that country, but not in excess of the taxes you would pay on the same income in the United States.

In many countries, real estate transactions are subject to a value-added tax (VAT), which is roughly equivalent to a flat tax. The VAT replaces high income taxes in some countries by distributing tax loads on goods, services, and investments. The Internal Revenue Service (IRS) does not consider a VAT to be an income tax, but it is deductible as an expense. It cannot be used as any part of the tax exclusion calculation.

Currency gains or losses that you incur when selling an investment are considered a capital gain or loss. A currency gain in connection with a trade or business or with the management or administration of investment assets is treated as an ordinary gain (rather than a capital gain), and any loss is generally treated as an expense.

Banking Outside the United States

When you invest in property outside the United States, you will likely need to establish an account in the local country to pay various expenses and to collect income. U.S. taxpayers may have foreign bank accounts, but if the account exceeds $10,000 at any time during the year, the IRS wants to know about it. The Bank Secrecy Act gave the Department of Treasury authority to establish record keeping and filing requirements for those with financial interests in or signature authority over accounts maintained with financial institutions in foreign countries. This provision requires that a Form TD F 90-22.1, Report of Foreign Bank and Financial Accounts (FBAR), be filed by the account holder by June 30 of each year. The FBAR rules were established to identify and track illicit funds or unreported income, as well as provide prosecutorial tools to combat money laundering and other crimes. A person in this regard can be a U.S. citizen or resident, domestic partnership or corporation, estate or trust, or a person living and doing business in the United States. Failing to file an FBAR report can result in civil and criminal penalties. Nonwillful negligence can be penalized up to $50,000, and willful violations can lead to higher penalties as well as criminal sentences.

There is no statute of limitations on unreported income. If the IRS finds out about some foreign bank account twenty years down the road, it's subject to penalties and interest plus the taxes that should have been paid. One audit is all that it takes. There is also no dollar threshold for tax evasion.

You must take seriously the necessity to report your accounts. Don't be like Benjie who thought he could outsmart the authorities but ended up caught for money laundering. Benjie directed my company, which was the custodian of his self-directed IRA, to move $1 million to a single-member limited liability company (LLC) on Nevis Island. Two years later, he closed his account stating that he had lost all the money in his investment venture. Then, once Benjie controlled the funds of his Nevis LLC, he wired the money to Canada and back again to Nevis. But Benjie didn't realize that he was creating a paper trail. Once funds move offshore, their movement is subject to more scrutiny. Banks may file a Suspicious Activity Report without informing you if they think there is any suspicious activity involved. Even transactions in small amounts, such as under $10,000, can be under scrutiny. Benjie didn't have a chance and now has some very serious problems, not the least of which are tax penalties on the early distribution of his retirement funds. The IRS considers the use of IRAs to launder money and evade taxes a growing concern; therefore, investment in LLCs managed by the beneficial owner of the IRA may be targets of more scrutiny in the future. We can thank the Benjies of the world for that.

Foreign Corporations

A U.S. taxpayer or U.S. company can own 100 percent of the stock of a "qualified" foreign corporation and not be required to pay any U.S. income taxes on any profits of that foreign corporation. To be a qualified foreign corporation, it must be incorporated in a U.S. possession or be domiciled in a country that has a comprehensive income tax treaty with the United States. A qualified foreign corporation may not have any passive investment income or any income from dealing on favorable terms with any U.S. shareholders or related persons. You can avoid these rules if five or fewer unrelated U.S. persons own no more than 50 percent of the corporation. Nonresident family members or foreign corporations who are shareholders are not included in this calculation. You must ensure that you organize the foreign corporation correctly to avoid the 50 percent rule and that the entity is not managed at all from within the United States. When constructed by a legal and tax professional, the foreign corporation may provide tax-deferral opportunities.

An international business company (IBC) is a corporation formed outside the United States that is usually exempt from tax in the country where it is formed, but it may not conduct any business in that country. For U.S. tax purposes, an IBC is treated the same as a foreign corporation. U.S. persons who form and own a foreign corporation or an IBC may elect to be treated as a partnership by filing Form 8832, Entity Classification.

A single-owner IBC may elect to be taxed as a disregarded entity. If an IBC receives more than 75 percent of its gross income from passive investment sources (interest, dividends, capital gains), it is deemed to be a passive foreign investment company (PFIC) and shareholders are required to pay current taxes on their share of the investment company income.

Estate and Gift Taxes

The U.S. estate and inheritance taxes are very complex if you own property in other countries. As a result, many U.S. taxpayers who own investments or businesses outside the country own those assets through a corporation. Although the owner of a corporation may die, the corporation does not; thus, there is no imposition of an estate tax in the country where the property is located. For a U.S. taxpayer, the value of the corporation stock would be included in his or her estate. The actual assets owned by the corporation, however, are not included separately by the estate, because those assets are already included within the value of the corporation's stock. But any assets, including real or personal property, located anywhere in the world, even the United States, owned by the deceased taxpayer will be included in the estate. For 2007 through 2008, there is an exemption of $2 million before the federal estate tax is imposed. For 2009, this amount increases to $3.5 million, and in 2010 the estate tax is repealed.

The countries that you have investments in will also have an impact on the amount of tax payable by your estate upon death. On the positive side, some countries have no inheritance tax. Other countries have complex rules or extremely high estate taxes, which may necessitate that your heirs sell the property to pay the taxes. The important thing is not to be caught off guard. Consult with local professionals and attorneys to understand what your options are before you purchase. There may be considerations regarding how the title is held that affect your estate and your beneficiaries. Unlike the United States, the country may be subject to religious laws and codes that affect inheritance. Or there may be rules that dictate who can inherit and in which order. For instance, in France, if title is held by you and your spouse and if you have children from any relationship, those children have priority over any other beneficiary, including your spouse. If you die in France but are a U.S. resident, the property you own in France is subject to French inheritance tax laws, which means your children have priority over your spouse. However, if you die outside of France, inheritance is based on the laws of the country of death. So as you can see, if you want to know where your estate is going and what taxes it may be subjected to, do your homework and seek legal counsel in the country that you are purchasing in.

In the End

The bottom line is that the Internal Revenue Code includes legal methods that you can use to avoid or minimize tax if you are investing outside the United States. In this regard, it is always best to consult with knowledgeable and competent tax advisors. When determining whether your investment is advantageous, you need to figure out the net operating income (NOI). On a global scale, income and the impact of taxation are intertwined. When you are making an investment in a country that does not tax your income, capital gains, or beneficiaries, you clearly have an advantage over one that does. Your NOI, so far is terrific. But in the context of your U.S. tax obligations, your NOI may not be as advantageous. In addition, if you want to repatriate funds earned in another country in the United States, there may be tax consequences. However, if you're making your investment with retirement funds, such as an IRA or 401(k), your investment can be tax deferred or even tax free—in the United States, that is. So let's now look at reducing your current and future tax burden by using retirement funds.

Using IRAs Offshore

An excellent way to minimize your tax obligation in the United States is to use your retirement funds to purchase real estate—either domestically or internationally. With a self-directed retirement plan, you can invest in rental property, rehabs, commercial property, raw land, and other forms of real estate. Once you have identified a truly self-directed custodian or administrator, the process is very simple and is basically like any other real estate transaction. One caveat, however, is that the tax-deferred or tax-free treatment of accounts such as IRAs is not recognized outside of the United States. You will still be obligated to pay the required taxes in the country of your investment. And this can never be said too many times: You should always consult a competent tax advisor who is well versed in international and U.S. tax application about your particular situation. What follows is just a quick look of what's involved using a self-directed IRA as an example; however, the basic rules and requirements apply to other types of retirement funds as long as they allow self-direction.

Self-Directed Accounts

To get started, the first thing you need to do is open a self-directed account and transfer or roll over funds from your existing retirement plans. When you find a piece of real estate that you would like to purchase, you direct your administrator to purchase the property *within* your IRA, just like you do when your IRA invests in mutual funds. You are not taking a taxable distribution from your IRA; you are simply making an investment within it. All the income from the investment goes back into your IRA, and all the expenses, such as maintenance and property taxes, are paid from the IRA.

The opportunity to invest tax-deferred, or even tax-free, through your retirement plan comes with some restrictions. Because the purpose of these accounts is to save for your retirement, you cannot use them for a current benefit. A current benefit would include using a property owned by your IRA as a vacation destination or second home. In addition, it is prohibited for your IRA to buy property from, sell or lease property to, or extend a loan to you or any disqualified person. Disqualified persons include you, your children, your parents, your spouse, and any business or trust owned or controlled by these people.

There are several ways you can approach investing in property with your retirement funds:

- Invest in real property directly by purchasing it with your IRA. The holder of the title is your IRA.
- Partner with your IRA. You can divide an investment according to each investor's contribution. You can partner with your personal funds or other people's IRAs or personal funds. This is a good method to use if the purchase amount exceeds what you have in your retirement fund. Each investor receives an undivided interest in the property, and all income is allocated directly in relationship to the amount invested by each person or IRA. You can even include yourself or family members as long as the transaction closes simultaneously.
- Leverage the investment. You can have leveraged property in your retirement account. The loan must be nonrecourse to you as an individual. There may be a tax on the income on the

amount financed, but this still can be an advantageous and worthwhile option.

- Set up a limited liability company (LLC) or land trust. Your IRA or plan can own interest in LLCs or be a beneficiary of land trusts. These entities then can purchase investment properties. This can be particularly advantageous when purchasing property offshore.

Roth vs. Traditional IRA

The tax advantages vary depending on whether you are using a Roth or traditional IRA. Traditional IRAs are tax deductible. Earnings grow tax free, but all withdrawals are taxed as income. You can start taking distributions without penalty at age fifty-nine and a half, and you are required to take distributions by April 1 of the year after you reach age seventy and a half. Withdrawals are taxed at your rate at the time of distribution. A traditional IRA may be a good choice if you expect your tax rate to be lower when you start taking withdrawals, especially if you invest the amount you deducted from your taxes when making your contribution, or if your level of income prevents you from contributing to a Roth IRA.

Roth IRAs are funded with post-tax earnings. Contributions to a Roth IRA are not tax deductible, but gains accumulate tax free and you do not pay tax on allowed distributions. The amount you can contribute is based on your modified adjusted gross income (AGI). You can contribute to a Roth regardless of your age. You can withdraw the funds after age fifty-nine and a half tax free if the assets have been in the IRA for at least five years, but unlike a traditional IRA, there are no minimum distribution requirements. You may prefer having a Roth IRA over a traditional IRA if you expect your tax rate at retirement to be the same or higher than your current tax rate, because your earnings and withdrawals are not taxed.

If you have a traditional IRA, you can convert it to a Roth IRA, which is considered a rollover. When you convert a traditional IRA to a Roth, you must pay the taxes due in the year of the rollover. The Tax Increase Prevention and Reconciliation Act, which was signed into law in 2006, eliminates the AGI ceiling of $100,000 for converting a traditional IRA to a Roth starting in 2010. There are no limits to the amount you can convert, and you can also choose whether to pay all the taxes due in 2010 or pay a portion of the amount owed in 2011 and 2012. Thereafter, you must pay the tax in the conversion year.

Selecting a Custodian or Trustee

For IRAs, the custodian or trustee is normally a bank, savings association, insurance company, or any other entity deemed by the Secretary of the Treasury to be able to carry out the responsibilities. Banks are permitted to use record keepers of their choice. Some banks that act as custodians for self-directed IRAs appoint record keepers and administrators to provide the administrative and ministerial requirements of customers. In all cases, the bank that is shown as the custodian is the legal custodian. The record keepers and administrators act as the agent for the custodian and provide you with the services that the custodian has contracted for.

The custodian, administrators, and record keepers should have a history of providing the kinds of services you are looking for so that you can review their track record. It is important to find out if the staff has specific knowledge about the investments you want to make.

Distributions

When you are eligible or required to take distributions, you can opt to receive either the entire sum or periodic distributions for the rest of your life. You can also take in-kind distributions. The taxable amount, if applicable, is based on the fair market value of the asset at the time of distribution. For example, Babette's and Peter's Roth IRAs each owned a 50 percent share of a flat in London. Because they were prohibited to use it, they leased it. The rent was paid to their IRAs, which also paid for all expenses. But when they turned sixty-five, they each took their share of the flat as a distribution without tax consequences. Now they are enjoying living in it themselves.

If your IRA owns assets offshore, determining the fair market value is not quite as straightforward. If you have real property, you will need to get an acceptable appraisal and have the amount converted to U.S. dollars. In the case of cash, the value of the currency being distributed must be established on the date of distribution in U.S. dollars. For required minimum distributions, the fair market value of the account is determined as of December 31 of the previous year. This information needs to be reported to the IRS, regardless of whether the IRA is a traditional or Roth. When distributing an offshore asset, timing is important because of fluctuating exchange rates, so select the day of distribution carefully.

Borrowing Money

IRAs and qualified plans can borrow funds, but the accounts themselves cannot be used as collateral for loans for personal use. The most difficult issue is finding a lender, because the loans must be nonrecoursive—financing where the property is the only collateral because you personally cannot be obligated to pay the note, according to the IRS code regarding trusts. A traditional loan provides for "recourse" to the borrower. In other words, if, for whatever reason, you can't make the mortgage payment, the lender reserves the right to come after you personally for the balance of the loan. In a nonrecourse loan, the cash flow from the property must be sufficient to cover the mortgage payment and all expenses because the lender cannot come back to you for any shortfalls.

Most institutional lenders won't lend to retirement plans because such loans cannot be resold in the secondary market through the usual network of mortgage bankers, brokers, and banks. Community banks and other portfolio lenders, such as hard-money or private lenders, are much more likely to make loans. Although you cannot guarantee the loan, a third party who is not related to you can. You can use other or additional collateral for the loan.

Obtaining nonrecourse loans in other countries is also difficult. Some countries treat them as commercial loans, which may be subject to different conditions. The complexity of dealing with trustees of retirement plans could delay matters and cause the seller to forego the transaction. In some cases, the lender may attempt to obtain personal guarantees aside from the loan made. Any such guarantees could cause the IRA to be subject to disqualification in the United States, but sometimes guarantees from unrelated third parties who are not disqualified persons are acceptable in foreign jurisdictions, just as they are in the United States. Working with a trustee that is familiar with international investments can help you make sure that you are working within the regulations.

Loan payments must be made by the retirement fund, either from the cash flow generated by the rental income or from existing funds in the account. If rental or other cash is not available, and the loan payment cannot be made, any payment made by a third party or by the IRA owner is automatically considered an excess contribution. Potentially, this may be considered a prohibited transaction.

If you do borrow money to purchase an asset, the debt financing is subject to unrelated business income tax (UBIT). "Debt-financed property" is an IRS term for a mortgage or loan against an asset, such as real estate. You also should be aware that the account might be taxed again when you begin taking distributions, unless you're using a Roth IRA, where all withdrawals are tax free.

Unrelated debt-financed income (UDFI) is profit made from borrowed funds. If your net income on all your debt-financed property exceeds $1,000 in a twelve-month period, the portion of the debt-financed property is subject to UBIT. However, if you no longer have a debt for the property in the year prior to a sale, your plan is not subject the UBIT, regardless of the amount of profit.

UBIT must be paid by the retirement plan. You can use funds from other IRAs or plans, but first you must transfer or roll over the funds to the IRA or plan with the debt. If you pay the debt with funds not in the retirement plan, it is considered an excess contribution and may be subject to penalty.

If you sell debt-financed property, you must include a percentage of any gain or loss when computing the UBIT. The percentage is that of the highest acquisition indebtedness of the property during the twelve-month period preceding the date of sale in relation to the property's average adjusted basis. The tax on this percentage of gain or loss is determined according to the usual rules for capital gains and losses. These amounts may be subject to the alternative minimum tax. If any part of the allowable capital loss is not taken into account in the current tax year, it may be carried back or carried over to another tax year without application of the debt/basis percentage for that year.

One way to avoid UBIT is to partner your IRA with other funds. If you use your IRA funds for the down payment and your personal funds for the mortgage, capital gains from a sale would be proportionately divided between you and the IRA. In this way, the debt financing was not incurred by the IRA. This approach is also a good way to get around the problem of lenders not wanting to give loans to a retirement fund. For example, let's say that you have a $100,000 property with a $20,000 interest vested to your IRA and $80,000 vested to you. The bank loans you the $80,000, and you personally make the payments. Any benefit from the purchase, such as rental income or income from a sale, is shared pro rata between you and the IRA. Expenses would be shared in the same way.

For a Future Retirement in Costa Rica

Sarah and Bill have a plan. They've heard about investment property in Costa Rica—beautiful locations, great weather, ease of living. And the best part: property is relatively inexpensive and easy to rent for a strong cash flow. They want to use their IRAs to fund their investments, but they also would like to live on their property after they retire. If they pool their IRAs, they will be able to buy a property outright, with each of their IRAs owning a portion based on the percentage contributed. If they want a bigger property, they can include friends in the deal. One way to make the transaction is to form an entity, such as a corporation or trust, to hold the property for the IRAs. The collective IRAs become stakeholders of the entity.

They head to Costa Rica to check it out. They have a great time exploring the country and taking side trips to look at real estate. Fortune is with them, and they find a property that they both agree on. Sarah and Bill each complete a buy direction letter to instruct the administrators of their IRAs to purchase the property. Their IRAs will take title once the transaction is complete. Their representatives must work with Costa Rican attorneys and title companies to ensure that the IRAs have ownership and that all income and expenses are properly credited and debited to their IRAs.

Sarah and Bill look into taking out a loan to buy the property. They discover that all debt used for acquiring property in any IRA must be nonrecourse. Usually a corporation or foundation is put together by legal counsel in Costa Rica, which will in turn be owned by the IRA. The corporation or foundation will then be the borrower, with property income and expense flowing through the IRA-owned Costa Rican entity. Any debt-financed property, regardless of where it is located, may be subject to unrelated debt-financed income tax in the United States.

The burn is that during the time that the property is owned by their IRAs, they can't live in it, not even for a moment. And neither can their parents, children, or children's spouses. Bill's older brother asked about renting the house for the winter. Although siblings are not specifically prohibited in the same manner as lineal descendents and ascendants, there are plenty of IRS rules that make living in a sibling's IRA-funded property a bad idea as well. A safer option is for Bill's brother to rent a nonrelated friend's property who also used an IRA for the purchase. In the meantime, Sarah and Bill's property is maintained by a property manager, and any maintenance must be performed by third parties unrelated to the couple.

When Sarah and Bill are ready to retire in six years to their Costa Rican property, they first need to take a complete distribution of the property owned by their IRAs, which becomes a taxable event for U.S. tax purposes. The fair market value of the property is added to their taxable income in the year of distribution. However, if they use Roth IRAs to purchase the property, they will not have to pay tax on the distribution. The distribution is a net asset value, so if Sarah and Bill have a debt against the property, the distribution amount will be based on the fair market value minus any mortgages. Any taxable distributions are reported on Form 1099-R.

Sarah and Bill's friend Louise finds their interest in Costa Rica infectious, especially after she joins them there for a vacation. She has a 401(k) with her employer and wants to know if she can use it for real estate investment just as Sarah and Bill did with their IRAs.

If Louise's workplace offers a self-directed 401(k), she can use it for such an investment, but it is unlikely that her employer's plan allows this. However, her plan may have an in-service withdrawal feature that permits her to roll over a portion of her vested funds to a self-directed IRA. Once Louise retires or quits, she can roll over her entire 401(k) plan to a self-directed IRA or a self-directed individual 401(k) plan and then purchase the Costa Rican property at her discretion.

Investment Examples

Now that we've gone over some of the nuts and bolts of offshore investing, let's look at a few other investors who have delved into the international arena. Each experience reveals different aspects of investing offshore, and the transactions are not necessarily specific to the country invested in. I have found that you learn something new each time you make an investment, and I have learned something from each of the personal accounts in the following chapters.

Returning Home to South Africa

Aleet grew up in the winelands of South Africa, a crosspatch of regions spreading out north, east, and south from the picturesque coastal city of Cape Town. At that time, South African wines were little known outside the country, and the troubles linked to apartheid were perhaps too well known. When a terrific career opportunity for her father beckoned in San Francisco, he moved the family there, including the sixteen-year-old Aleet.

Aleet's connection to South Africa didn't end though. Her family kept their South African home and returned many times for vacations to enjoy the region's temperate, almost Mediterranean climate. But while Aleet revisited childhood memories, the nation of South Africa was moving decidedly forward. The policy of apartheid was finally dismantled in 1989, free elections in 1994 led to Nelson Mandela's presidency, and the Truth and Reconciliation Committee was set up to try and foster a peaceful transition from a complicated past to a prosperous, integrated future. One striking symbol of South Africa joining the world has been its increasing reputation for exporting notable wines from the regions of Aleet's youth. In addition, the nation received tremendous prestige upon being awarded the opportunity to host the 2010 World Cup, soccer's most visible event.

The adult Aleet became a United States citizen, and over the years developed into an astute real estate investor in her new country. She built up personal savings, as well as her 401(k) and IRA. Considering the positive changes in her native South Africa, it shouldn't come as a surprise that she has decided to apply her real estate know-how to the country she never completely left.

Aleet's particular interest is to invest in city apartments along the coast in the Cape Town area. She believes such an investment could provide a real income opportunity for her, as well as bolster her retirement accounts. But she is aware that real estate is a thorny issue in South Africa, because even more than a decade and a half after apartheid, whites still own most of the nation's land. Nonetheless, she has been encouraged by recent statements from the South African government, as noted in a December 8, 2006, report by Reuters. The country's president, Thabo Mbeki, had ordered a probe into property prices, fearing that an influx of wealthy foreigners into the nation's real estate market would drive prices out of the reach of many South Africans. Government spokesman Themba Maseko had particularly singled out the possible curbing of the sale of prime coastal land to foreigners, which would have signaled South Africa's first official move to block nonresidents from buying real estate there. But only a few days later, Maseko retracted his earlier statement: "There will be no ban on foreign ownership. It was entirely my mistake."

Cape Town vs. Elsewhere

Aleet begins her research mindful of three considerations: her nonresident status, tax issues regarding offshore real estate, and the attractiveness of Cape Town versus other cities in Europe and elsewhere. Her strategy is twofold: (1) to buy a property to her best advantage with regard to South African taxes, since she will be taxed on her worldwide income, and (2) to defer tax on income by using her retirement funds.

Although Aleet grew up in South Africa, she is a nonresident. Although there still are no restrictions on property ownership by nonresidents, there are procedures and requirements that must be followed. As a nonresident, Aleet can buy real estate either directly in her own name or via a legal holding entity, such as a trust or corporation. Some investors prefer the latter method for taxation as well as management and asset protection purposes. But because Aleet wants to use her IRA and 401(k) funds, she really has no choice but to use a legal entity. United States tax law prohibits her from making the investment in her own name if she is using retirement funds. In her research, she discovers that a non–South African entity must register locally in South Africa when it buys property in the country. Furthermore, local companies that have shares owned by a nonresident must have a public officer who is a resident of South Africa. If a nonresident plans to reside in the country for longer periods, that person must apply for permanent residency. This is not an issue for Aleet, who has no immediate plans of living in South Africa.

Aleet recognizes that she has an emotional draw to South Africa, but if she puts on her business hat, she knows that it is important to investigate how attractive Cape Town is in comparison to real estate investment opportunities elsewhere in the world. While staying in Cape Town and working with a South African agent who has been active in real estate for decades, she discovers that cash-flowing rental properties are available in the city. She learns that the methods of property ownership are either freehold or leasehold, and that the majority of properties bought by nonresidents are leasehold, making the rules relating to the use of that property far more flexible.

Her initial research comes up with the following figures for various areas of the city, broken down into cost per square meter to allow for ready comparison. (At the time of this writing, one United States dollar is worth about 7.2 rand. For example, $10,000 equals about R72,000. The conversions supplied below are approximate.) In the more pricey buildings situated in prime locations, a two-bedroom apartment sells for about R32,000 per square meter, whereas less opulent complexes have apartments at about R16,000 to R18,000 per square meter. In other nearby areas, Aleet finds sea-facing apartments on the market for R20,000 to R25,000.

So how does this compare with other parts of the world? After converting all amounts from other currencies into the South African rand, Aleet realizes that a similar apartment in the prime locales of the sixth and seventh arrondissements of Paris would be about R91,000 per square meter, almost three times the priciest apartments in Cape Town. Chelsea in London isn't much better at R88,000, nor for that matter is New York's Upper East Side at R82,000. Prices are comparable in Madrid. Closer to where she is looking, she finds that in Durban, a coastal city on the Indian Ocean side of South Africa, the most expensive apartments are R14,000.

After doing her due diligence, Aleet feels confident that she is making the right decision. Cape Town is an attractive city that is affordable to her with a lot of potential, and her research shows that properties would hold their value.

Preparing for the Purchase

Aleet locates a perfect rental property in Cape Town for R1,750,000, but she wants to be sure that the property will provide enough cash flow to cover taxes and maintenance expenses. Based on the advice she receives from her local advisor, she can get about 9–10 percent of the property's value per month as a rental. To achieve a 5 percent return, she figures she would need at least a 50 percent loan to value. The property already had a renter who was paying R14,000 a month. According to the law, a buyer must honor an existing rental agreement.

Because Aleet wants to buy the property with her IRA and 401(k) funds, the actual buyer will be SA Holdings LLC, which she established with those funds. As a nonresident entity, her American LLC must be converted to a private company as a condition of purchase. Aleet finds a conveyancer, which is a specially qualified legal practitioner for handling the details of transfer, to establish the legal holding entity that will buy the property. The conveyancer represents her in the purchase, carries out all title and land registry searches and checks, and ensures that all documents and agreements are properly handled. South Africa is reputed to have one of the best deed registration systems in the world, with an exceptionally high degree of accuracy.

Aleet makes the offer to purchase via her corporation and places a deposit of R175,000. A deposit isn't mandatory but serves as a good faith gesture and reassures the seller of Aleet's financial wherewithal. The conveyancer invests the deposit in an interest-bearing trust account for the benefit of SA Holdings, the entity she registered in South Africa.

The seller's conveyancer prepares the transfer documentation, which will be recorded along with the cancellation of any existing mortgage bonds at the regional Deeds Registry. These deeds are subject to an intense examination process, after which they will be made available for registration. When a deed is transferred, any liabilities incurred by the previous owner remain with the previous owner, unless otherwise agreed upon.

Now to the contractual nitty-gritty. In South Africa, all real estate contracts must be in writing, contain certain prescribed information, and be signed by both buyer and seller to be valid and legally binding. Contracts most commonly take the form of an Agreement of Sale, or an Offer to Purchase that once accepted constitutes an Agreement of Sale. An Agreement of Sale signed by both parties represents a valid and binding document from which neither party can withdraw without incurring legal consequences, except for specific instances where the agreement is not fulfilled. The closing will be in forty-five days, during which time all searches and inspections must be completed and funds made ready.

The purchase agreement guarantees the balance of the purchase price. In general, such a guarantee is only acceptable if it is issued by a local financial institution. Aleet needs to make an arrangement between her custodial bank in the United States and a local bank for a back-to-back guarantee to be issued. Because Aleet plans to purchase future properties in South Africa, she transfers funds for the current and potential future deals from her SA Holdings LLC account in the United States to SA Holdings. If a purchase is contingent on obtaining a mortgage, it must be detailed in the purchase agreement.

South Africa has specific exchange control restrictions that apply to nonresident purchasers when remitting funds to South Africa or repatriating funds overseas for the resale of real estate. For the most part, any property investor who remains a nonresident can remit and repatriate funds freely. Additionally, a nonresident can repatriate any capital gains made after the owed taxes are deducted.

And then there are other important details to go over. "As is where is" is a standard inclusion in all deeds of sale, which means that the property is bought "as is," that is to say, "in the exact condition in which the property is found." All defects within the seller's knowledge must be disclosed. Generally, surveys are not conducted on South African properties, but they may be arranged and can be included as a conditional part of the purchase agreement. The law requires property owners to possess a valid "electrical compliance certificate," which verifies that the electrical installations at the property meet certain safety statutes. A "beetle-free certificate" declares all accessible portions of the property free of infestation by certain defined beetles, although this certificate is not required for apartments and thus is not a concern for Aleet. The seller pays for both of these certificates, unless another arrangement is mutually agreed to. All fixtures and fittings, which include anything attached to the property, are part of the purchase, and if there is any doubt, an inventory should be included.

Aleet looks into getting a mortgage. In South Africa, a nonresident can borrow only up to the maximum of the amount invested in the property purchase, which translates to a 50 percent to value borrowing ratio. Such loans are also subject to foreign exchange approval by the South African Reserve Bank. Because Aleet is using retirement funds for the purchase, SA Holdings would be liable for unrelated business income tax. She decides to keep debt financing out of the purchase.

Coming to a Close

It's deal day. If this real estate transaction had been done outside of South Africa, the documentation pertaining to the registration of the transfer of property would need to be signed in black ink and notarized or otherwise authenticated. Aleet has avoided the issue by forming SA Holdings and then providing her conveyancer with power of attorney to conclude the purchase on behalf of SA Holdings.

The seller usually pays any brokerage fees, but SA Holdings is responsible for the transfer costs. The government levies a transfer duty, which is a variable rate tax between 1 percent and 8 percent for private ownership, and 10 percent for purchase via a legal entity such as a trust. Transfer costs will be around 1–2 percent. The conveyancer's fees for attending to the transfer and registration are calculated according to a tariff. Further sundry charges are imposed by the Deeds Registry and by the bank if borrowed funds are involved. The rental deposit from the inherited renter is also transferred to Aleet's SA Holdings account.

Once the Income Starts to Flow

Aleet has now achieved her goal—she is a property owner in the country of her youth. Her foray into the worldwide real estate market has been exciting, but she is also aware of two less-exciting prospects on the horizon: income tax and capital gains.

Nonresidents are taxed on income derived from a South African source, and thus Aleet as SA Holdings must register as a South African taxpayer. Rental income from a South African property is taxed and included in the taxpayer's gross income. Tax deductions can be claimed for operating expenses, including repairs and maintenance, interest costs, and agent's commissions for administering the property. No income tax deduction can be claimed for the cost of the property purchase. Improvements to the property and transfer costs (including conveyance fees) also are not tax deductible. Only 25 percent of any capital gains is included in the nonresident's taxable income.

In terms of capital gains, the tax rates vary depending on whether the property is owned directly by an individual nonresident or by a nonresident company or trust. The maximum capital gains tax rate for a nonresident individual is 10 percent. Should Aleet sell the property, capital gains tax is levied on the difference between the property's base cost and the sale price. The cost of the purchase of the property, transfer costs, and improvements to the property are added to the base cost for the purposes of the capital gains tax. Borrowing costs, including interest and points, and costs for repairs, maintenance, and insurance usually are not added to the base cost.

Looking to the Future

Before we leave Aleet, who is toasting the completion of her first successful purchase in South Africa with a world-class glass of chenin blanc from the Stellenbosch region, let's look to the future. If Aleet decides to retire in South Africa, as a nonresident buyer, her application for residency would take into account that she's already invested in property in the country. Once she becomes a resident, she may only remit and repatriate funds for five years, after which she must abide by the exchange control restrictions that are imposed on South African residents. If anything unfortunate should happen to Aleet, her property would be liable to estate duty.

France: The Necessity of a Notaire

Whether it's a pied-à-terre in Paris or an old farmhouse in Provence, France is an attractive investment destination for many. France never lacks for admirers in the United States and elsewhere, so despite the high ticket price, it remains a good area to invest in. For anyone thinking of buying property anywhere in France, the first thing to do is to find a notaire. Despite the recent development of real estate agents, especially in major cities, notaires continue to be the principal partners of any real estate transaction in France. They will help you find a property and have a monopoly over preparing the deed and overseeing the necessary legal aspects.

But before we examine the important role of the notaire, let's take a look at two different approaches to purchasing an apartment in Paris, the first as an individual, the second as a corporate entity, both using the services of Philip Gordon of MDG-France, an architect who has been working in Paris for many years. For an established fee, Philip helps clients refine their criteria for real estate investment and then guides them in finding the desired property. He also assists in establishing a proper banking relationship in France, both for debt financing and to ensure conformity with U.S. tax laws and reporting. His team includes rehabbers and a maintenance crew, so that permanent residents or renters are properly cared for once the properties are acquired.

A Parisian Retirement

Bruce has visited France numerous times and long ago decided that Paris is one of the great cities of the world. Rather than just dream about it, Bruce has an enviable twenty-year plan: buy a cash-flowing property in Paris with Roth IRA funds, and upon retirement in two decades, move into it.

Bruce initiates his plan by contacting Philip Gordon of MDG-France, who finds Bruce several apartments in highly desirable arrondissements (the French equivalent of a district) that fit his needs, one of which would not require much additional capital for rehabbing, to Bruce's delight. It also appears likely to meet Bruce's goal of a cash return of 6 percent. The apartment is about eighty square meters, with desirable amenities such as a fireplace and an additional bedroom. It's definitely somewhere Bruce can see himself living comfortably twenty years hence.

Philip estimates that the apartment will need about €20,000 in improvements, which added to the purchase price would bring Bruce's total initial investment to about €710,000. He further estimates that the apartment could bring in about €40,000 annually, factoring in €4,500 for taxes and maintenance.

At Philip's suggestion, Bruce opens an account at Barclays Bank to transact income and expense business, for which he presents identification and a W-9. Because the account is likely to exceed $10,000 in any given year, he also will need to report it to the IRS on Form TD F 90-22.1 (Report of Foreign Bank and Financial Accounts) by June 30 of the following year.

Here we leave the specifics of Bruce's case, whose all-cash acquisition will be consummated smoothly. Now let's look at how Sidney and Susanne turned their knowledge into a successful business investment.

A Parisian Business

Sidney and Susanne have bought and sold commercial properties throughout the world, but their sights are now set on France, for personal as well as financial reasons. From an investment perspective, France is a stable country with a long-established political and social system, and as part of the European Union (EU), it uses the dependable euro. But the couple also has family reasons for their interest across the Atlantic: not only do they spend a lot of time in France, speak French, and admire the French culture, but also and more importantly, their children live in France and are interested in investing there themselves.

Sidney and Susanne decide to make the opening plunge into the Parisian real estate market and then pass on what they learn from the process to their children. Sidney is currently a Canadian resident and taxpayer as well as a U.S. taxpayer, and Susanne is a U.S. resident and taxpayer. They want noncommercial properties to add to their retirement nest egg, whereas their children will be more concerned with income and cash flow.

The couple's game plan focuses on individual investor apartments. Because property in Paris is at a premium, they enlist the help of Philip, who has been recommended to them with highest praise thanks to their children's research. Had they lacked the benefit of family eyes and ears in France to do some of the preliminary legwork for them, Sidney and Susanne also could have considered using a notaire at this early stage, because some notaires have real estate departments. There also are many professional real estate agencies in France—*immobiliers*—and some of them have international skills, but *immobiliers* only represent sellers, and in fact over 60 percent of all residential sales in the country are conducted by individuals rather than real estate agents.

After a thorough search with Philip, Sidney and Susanne determine that the cost of a flat in Paris is anywhere from €4,000 to €20,000 per square meter, depending on such factors as arrondissement, building style (ancien, Haussmanian, modern, and so on), the condition of the unit and building, and nearness to amenities. They want an apartment that is already furnished, primarily because evictions are less thorny when a flat is furnished. Judicial proceedings are necessary when evicting someone from an unfurnished flat.

Philip discusses with the couple some pertinent details regarding their prospective investment. Property tax is determined by the local Parisian authorities, but the tax is relatively minor compared with higher rates in the provinces. There is an annual occupancy tax that is paid by the renter and typically added to the rent. Depending on the arrangement, administration and property management fees can be paid by either the landlord or the tenant.

How Sidney and Susanne choose to structure their investment will affect the tax implications. For instance, if they purchase the unit through a corporation, they must annually declare the names of the shareholders. If they don't declare the shareholder names, they must pay 3 percent of the purchase price annually. To purchase the property as individuals, it is crucial that they determine the rights of heirs with regard to the vesting of title. If they decide to debt-finance any of the purchase, life insurance is typically required for the amount of the loan, with the lending bank as the beneficiary. For the sale of the property down the road, non-EU residents pay 33 percent on capital gains, whereas EU residents pay 16 percent. After ten years and after fifteen years, the capital gains tax decreases significantly both for residents and nonresidents.

Now that Sidney and Susanne, with Philip's invaluable assistance, are acquainted with the ins and outs of Paris real estate, they present Philip with an additional consideration. Having decided against debt financing, they want to use cash from their IRAs and 401(k)s, both of which are trusts housed in entities that in effect make them corporations. Philip recommends that the acquisition be done through a Societe Commerciale Immobilier (SCI), and he helps them form such an entity with the assistance of the couple's French legal counsel.

Here's how the SCI transaction works. Sidney and Susanne form a LLC in the United States owned exclusively by their retirement funds. Then their self-directed IRAs and 401(k)s fund the SCI via a money transfer from the LLC to the SCI account at Barclays Bank in France. They could choose to fund the SCI directly with their IRAs and 401(k)s, but handling it through the LLC makes things less complicated should they eventually decide to live in France. In addition to the purchase price itself, the funding amount from the LLC to SCI takes into account renovation costs, maintenance, taxes, and other costs associated with the SCI and the property it would own.

The SCI fully discloses its owners (the LLC; the IRAs and 401(k)s as owners of the LLC; and Sidney and Susanne as owners of the IRAs and 401(k)s). This avoids any taxation based on corporate ownership in France. The SCI is responsible for filing tax reports in France. In the United States, Sidney's and Susanne's retirement funds and LLC must file Form TD F 90-22.1, Report of Foreign Bank and Financial Accounts.

And now, let's look into how Sidney and Susanne and Bruce complete their transactions with the very important individual anyone wishing to invest in real estate must get to know—the notaire.

Introducing the All-Powerful Notaire

The notaire is not merely the first and last name regarding real estate transactions in France; the notaire is essentially the *only* name. The notaire is both a public official, granted powers by the French government, and legal counsel. No deal is done without a notaire, and virtually none of those deals are disputed—contract litigation concerning real estate transactions is very rare in France. There are about 7,200 notaires currently in office.

The notaire's professional fee is fixed by law, and neither the notaire nor the client can modify this fee. If the seller and buyer each retain a notaire, the two notaires share the established fee, and no fee increase is allowed. If the notaire is used as a consultant outside of the legally prescribed duties, those fees are determined by a separate agreement between the notaire and the client. Currently, the notaire's fee is 5 percent of the purchase price for the first €45,735, and 2.5 percent for any amount over that. This fee is subject to 19.6 percent VAT. These amounts are due only when the transaction is concluded.

The notaire has the following powers:

- Counsels clients on real estate matters anywhere in France without jurisdictional restrictions
- Verifies title of the property
- Requests a survey of the property and informs the prospective buyer of any applicable local planning regulations, easements, or common-use areas that may have an impact on the property
- Drafts and authenticates deeds
- Ensures that the parties to the transaction are legal persons or entities and that they are capable of closing the deal as per the agreement
- Supervises the paying off of any existing debt
- Presides over the final sales agreement, which is virtually un-challengeable in court
- Records the sale

Let's look at these one by one.

Counseling clients. There is no legal necessity to use a notaire at this stage. In fact, Bruce, Sidney, and Susanne chose to use Philip rather than a notaire when looking for properties, because he knew the local market and could quickly facilitate finding what they were looking for. About 60 percent of all real estate sales are initiated by individuals rather than real estate agents, but some notaires have a real estate department that provides assistance in locating properties. The advantage of bringing in a notaire early is that their overall knowledge of real estate transactions in France is unrivaled. Many also can provide insight into the particulars of specific locales, based on their familiarity through past transactions and general knowledge, and they can be particularly helpful with respect to tenant rights when an investor is considering the purchase of a rental property in a rural area. Notaires are also the only officials who have access to the valued Perval files, which list the sales price of every real estate transaction executed in France.

Technically, the notaire does not have to be involved at the Promise of Sale stage. A lawyer or real estate agent may sign this document, which is a nonbinding contract between the seller and buyer. In fact, some sellers simply use the document to shop around for a higher price from another buyer. However, it is important to understand that all future obligations of the parties rely on the Promise of Sale, which fixes the commitments of the parties. Because of this, a notaire's advice is very useful during the Promise of Sale negotiations so that a party does not end up making a commitment without realizing the full consequences down the road.

The Promise of Sale stipulates, among other things, the details and state of the property, the existing encumbrances, the price and terms of payment, the amount of the security deposit, the date for taking possession, and any other conditions that the buyer wishes to include (building permit, mortgage, and so on). After a "cooling period" of seven business days, during which the buyer can back out for any reason, the buyer places a deposit equal to 10 percent of the purchase price with the notaire, which in essence guarantees the buyer's commitment. If the buyer either cannot or does not wish to continue with the purchase, the deposit is awarded to the seller. If the seller dies after the buyer has placed the deposit with the notaire, the heirs of the seller must finalize the purchase or lose the deposit.

Verifying title. The notaire is authorized to conduct the title search and to verify title. The buyer is provided a relatively detailed history of the property, which must go back at least thirty years and may go back as far as the original construction of the property and include surveys extending more than a century into the past. The statute of limitations for real estate transactions is thirty years. Notaires must keep records of real estate transactions and related deeds for 100 years after their execution.

Investigating property details. The notaire requests a survey of the property, which becomes part of the final sales agreement. The surveyor hired by the notaire is responsible and liable for the information provided in the survey. The notaire also researches applicable local planning regulations, as well as determines whether any easements or common-use areas are involved, and then must inform the buyer of any related consequences with regard to the purchase. If the buyer wishes to build on or change the use of the property, a permit process is instituted that may add many months to the overall transaction. Ordinarily, any of these modifications will be established prior to the signing of the sales agreement.

Drafting and authenticating contracts. The notaire is solely responsible for drafting and authenticating the contracts for the real estate transaction, and once authenticated, the contracts are considered virtually indisputable in court. The notaire also provides complete security for these contracts. In light of this power, the notaire must exercise extreme caution before authenticating any contract. Any professional mistake committed by the notaire is immediately penalized by a judge and the notaire is held liable. For this reason, notaires are insured, thereby providing a financial guarantee to the client. Most contracts are signed in France by all the relevant parties, but this is not a legal necessity; a notaire may send a contract anywhere to be signed. The contract must be published in France, however, to be considered legally enforced.

All real estate sales agreements must be drafted in French, and using a foreign language in such deeds is illegal. Some notaires with international experience may translate the agreements for their clients.

Verifying legality and capability of parties. It is the notaire's exclusive responsibility to determine that the parties to the transaction are legal persons or entities and that they are able to enter into such an agreement. Further, the law governing real property transactions states that the notaire is liable for issues arising from the agreement. If, for example, the buyer is unable to close due to lack of funds, the notaire could be liable to the seller for potential damages.

Supervising debt payoff. The notaire is responsible for determining whether there is an outstanding debt or other encumbrance on the property. The Mortgage Registry is consulted to determine the status of any mortgage on the property. Its outstanding mortgage statement (also known as the payoff amount) is valid for two months after the figure is given to the notaire. The notaire then pays off the existing debt from the funds held by the notaire as part of the settlement prior to crediting the proceeds of the sale to the seller.

By the way, the concept of the mortgage was originally conceived in France, so it probably goes without saying that mortgage loans (including nonrecourse loans) are available from most any French bank. Often the notaire provides advisory services to banks and buyers regarding the best structure of the loan and method of guarantee for repayment. The security agreement, almost always drafted by the notaire, usually takes the form of a mortgage.

Producing the final agreement. After the notaire has completed all of the above steps, which typically takes at least three months, the parties sign the final agreement. This agreement, called the *contract fini* or the *acte authentique*, is for all intents and purposes unassailable in court. It takes about two months for the sale to be registered.

Recording the sale. At closing, the notaire receives the final payment for the purchase, and in turn pays any outstanding debt, taxes, or other secured creditor. Then the notaire records ownership in the name of the buyer, and the seller is cleared from title as well as from all secured creditors or other individuals who have claims against the property. All transfer taxes are paid by the notaire with proceeds from the seller.

For new construction or for a building that is being sold less than five years after being completed, a real estate VAT of 19.6 percent is included in the deed of sale. Because VAT is only paid once for the same property, there is a tax credit that can be repaid upon the sale of the building. Reconstruction of existing commercial versus residential structures has different ramifications for VAT. The real estate VAT is one of the most complex aspects of the French tax system, and the notaire should certainly be consulted.

Money Matters

Three annual taxes must be paid. A real estate tax must be paid by all owners, whether private individuals or companies. The amount is calculated based on the total surface area of the property. A residential tax is paid by the occupants, based on a measurement of the occupied area. This tax differs from one locale to another, though generally the differences are not large. It should be noted, however, that the residential tax is the only source of revenue for some municipalities, and it may actually exceed the real estate tax. A professional tax is only paid by companies; it is based on factors such as the company's revenues and number of employees.

Any rental revenue from a property owned by a nonresident is considered income. In France, the average income tax rate is 25 percent, so it might be more advantageous for a nonresident to declare the income in France. Capital gains tax on the sale of real estate property for non-EU residents is 33 percent, compared to 16 percent for EU residents. Non-EU persons must have a banking relationship in the EU to confirm the payment of such capital gains tax. Capital gains tax is reduced depending on the number of years you own the property; property speculation is not encouraged. If a transaction does not generate any capital gain, an exemption may be required from the tax authorities.

The notaire—we always seem to be coming back to the notaire— may advise investors on all tax filing rules, including the capital gains tax rates, and may execute tax filings for investors.

The Final Transaction

France's inheritance taxes for spouses and nonspouse beneficiaries can be very high, so planning is essential. This may involve using companies to hold the property as shareholders. The failure to plan for French inheritance taxes may result in having to sell the property to pay the taxes.

Children are entitled to inherit property before a spouse. Inheritance works in this way:

- Neither a husband nor wife is considered a legal heir.
- If you are survived by one child, you can give up to one-half of your French property to third parties.
- If you are survived by two children, you can give up to one-third of your French property to third parties.
- If you are survived by three or more children, you can give up to one-fourth of your French property to third parties.
- Children can renounce their reserved rights but only after the death of a parent.

If you have no children, other members of your family may qualify as legal heirs and, therefore, have mandated rights to a proportion of the property.

If a surviving spouse lives in a property at the time of the death, the spouse can live in the home for one year free of cost, and the estate of the deceased pays all the costs. If the property was solely owned by the couple, the surviving spouse has the right to live in the property and the right to use the home furnishings for the rest of his or her life.

Offshore trusts holding investments may avoid French succession law, because French courts cannot access assets not located in France if they are held in an offshore trust. SCI shares can be left to heirs based on the laws of the legal residence of the beneficiaries. SCI shares are not subject to French inheritance law but are subject to inheritance taxes.

If you are not a French resident, inheritance tax is payable only on assets located in France. The inheritance tax is paid by each beneficiary, pro rata on the net asset value of the property.

French inheritance tax can be reduced when owners gift their real property to their children while retaining the lifetime right of occupancy. The methodology is straightforward, but as is everything under the inheritance laws, the amount of tax avoided is dependent on age as well as tax discounts. As said before, seek legal counsel.

7

Panama for Sale

If you do an online search on buying real estate in Panama, the over tens of thousands of sites will entice you with the merits of this popular destination. Of course, there is the famous fifty-mile-long canal, one of the great human enterprises, of which the United States relinquished complete control to Panama in 2000 and will reach the 100th anniversary of its historic opening in 2014. Then there are its location and geography. A short plane ride from the United States brings you to beautiful islands and beaches for sunning and scenery. Everywhere in Panama is fairly close to water, with the Caribbean to the north and the gulfs of Panama and Chiriqui to the south. In many of the highland and midland areas, the climate is relatively temperate year-round. In addition, the country is affordable and modern, and it has a booming real estate market. It is hardly surprising that many non-Panamanians have emigrated there to retire. But before we explore the nitty-gritty of Panamanian real estate investments, let's begin with a reminder of how important it is to get to know the country you're interested in before putting any of your money into it.

The Importance of Title

Boquette is a mountain town situated in a valley formed by an extinct volcano and highly regarded as one of Panama's premium

coffee-growing areas. Because of its pleasant climate and scenic locale, not to mention its flavorful coffee, it has become a destination
for tourists and, more recently, retirees.

Sam, an American developer, did everything right in Boquette.
He made the proper connections with the local and central government authorities, and above all *he obtained clear title* through a reputable law firm to some very choice real estate. There he built homes
for US$200,000 to US$350,000 in a gorgeous forest setting, adding
an eighteen-hole golf course. Overall, the amenities were not too
different from those offered in upscale U.S. retirement communities,
but they were a fraction of the cost. He sold every one of the homes
to buyers who either live there, use their homes as cash-flowing
properties, or have already made money reselling their appreciated
real estate. In other words, Sam's experience is a success story from
beginning to end.

In contrast, Ron went about it the wrong way. Ron's story gets a
lot more space here, because often the better lessons are learned
from what one shouldn't do. Ron is a jovial, engaging person, the
classic "can-do" kind of guy. He also is a real estate investor, and it
wasn't long after he discovered Boquette that he wanted to acquire
some prime property for a housing development with incredible
mountain views. The area consisted of farms on which an indigenous group resided. Once he arranged to pay them for their properties and move them out, he would begin his dream development.

Marta and Grace are U.S. citizens. Marta emigrated from Panama
about forty years ago, but after she inherited her mother's property
in Panama, she went back frequently to vacation. Both she and
Grace are old hands at foreign property investment, and so it was
natural that eventually, at Marta's urging, they would aim their investing radar at Panama.

A mutual acquaintance introduced them to Ron, who drove them
in his Land Rover over ancient roads to the prime Boquette property,
with incredible vistas that extended all the way to the sea on a clear day.
A tractor stood by, prepared to begin road improvements, although

awaiting repairs. He offered them a special deal. For a $6,000 good faith down payment by check, they could purchase a one-hectare parcel of prime Boquette land, with the remaining $54,000 due upon titling of the property.

Marta and Grace couldn't help but notice that the indigenous residents were currently farming the property. Ron assured them that they had already been paid for the land and would soon move. Further, he promised he would not cash the check until titling was perfected. He said that he already knew of a number of people who would pay $85,000 for the parcels, so the women could make an immediate profit if they wished to sell soon afterward.

To further reassure them, Ron arranged for them to place their good faith check with Ignacio, a highly regarded property and business lawyer in Panama City whom Marta already knew and trusted. Ignacio told them that the check would become nonnegotiable after ninety days should Ron fail to provide title. After about a month, Marta and Grace contacted Ignacio to see how things were progressing. Obviously, not as well as Ron had envisioned.

First, Ron was having problems with Boquette's mayor with regard to the projected road improvements. But that was small potatoes compared to the major problem: Although the indigenous residents had never perfected their property interests, they were in fact legitimate owners of the property. The cost of perfecting a property interest was about $1,500, which most indigenous people didn't make in five years! Some of the property in question was listed in very old record books, and a proper title search could take months.

Three months later, Marta and Grace's check was no longer negotiable, and Ron still did not have title. Unlike Sam, he continued to do things his own way rather than the way things were done in Boquette. Ignacio let Marta and Grace know that he was no longer representing Ron. Now, over two years after Ron's initial proposal to the women, the local residents still farm on the prime mountainside land, *and* they've gained some better roads in the bargain.

Two Kinds of Property: Titled and Possession Rights

There are two primary approaches to foreign investment in real estate in Panama: the purchase of a titled property, which is applicable to land duly recorded and titled with the Public Registry, and the purchase of a "possession right." Possession rights are basically land-use acknowledgments that are recognized based on the occupation and use of a particular property over time and are granted only for a predetermined length of time.

Possession Rights: Buyer Beware

Not all properties in Panama are in the private domain. Many beachfront properties, islands, and real estate in special tourism zones and historically protected areas are owned and managed by the national or local municipal governments. In those areas, possession rights are granted for a determined period of time. Two such protected areas are the archipelago of Bocas del Toro (mouth of the bull), which to many visitors fits the description of tropical paradise, and Portobelo, a beautiful harbor on the Caribbean visited by Columbus and the final resting place of Sir Francis Drake. Some beachfront property is available for purchase but is subject to the law that all beaches are public. All beachfront properties must provide a right of way starting twenty-two lineal meters from the highest tide to the property line.

Because of the lack of uniformity regarding the granting of possession rights, possession rights should be approached with caution. When considering properties located in such areas, you should ensure that the possession right has in fact been granted by the relevant national or local government authorities and that the length of the time right is adequate for the purpose of the investment. The possession right should also contain a complete description of the property, including boundaries, encumbrances, and any other significant features or details (with an accompanying complete blueprint drawn and approved). You should make sure that any anticipated construction, activity, or improvement is acceptable by the national or local government. Transferring a possession right can take up to six months, depending on many factors, such as the date of recognition of the possession right and inspection by the granting entity.

Purchasing Titled Property

Nonresidents may purchase titled property in Panama. However, article 121 of the Panamanian Tax Code establishes that foreign persons or Panama corporations with foreign ownership cannot purchase property located less than ten kilometers from the frontiers or from islands under the jurisdiction of Panama.

Panama has a reliable Public Registry Office, which keeps records of all titled properties in each of the nine provinces and is founded on the land registration system inherited from Spain. The office is entrusted with identifying and making known to the general public—through its records—all property and rights over real estate with respect to an identified parcel of land (which include ownership, mortgages, easements, priorities, and certain types of tenancies). A national cadastral office, the Catastro, is the land registry from which all properties in Panama are indexed. (A "cadastre" is an official registry of the quantity, value, and ownership of real estate used to figure taxes. "Catastro" sounds unnervingly close to "catastrophe"; the two words are not linguistically related, but at tax time they may seem to be.)

Another key player with regard to registering land is the notary. The notary, whose services are usually paid for by the buyer, does not act as counsel to any of the parties in the transaction. The notary's primary function is to ensure that the transaction is carried out pursuant to law.

A third key player is the buyer's counsel. This lawyer must carry out an extensive investigation of Public Registry Office records with regard to the chain of title as well as any liens existing on the property. Once the purchase-and-sale transaction has been closed and the public deed has been signed by the notary, the buyer's counsel is responsible for registering the public deed with the Public Registry Office.

A real estate right is not finalized until the transaction is registered with the Public Registry. The registration also makes these rights known to third parties, and thus the rights can then be asserted against such third parties. Because the Panama system is a first-come, first-serve system, the recordation also affects the priority of liens placed on interest in real estate and is not dependent on the date of closing.

Before purchasing a property in Panama, a nonresident investor must take the following steps. The investor must perform complete due diligence of the property, which includes a complete title search, review of cadastral maps, and verification that the land is in good standing with regard to payment of taxes, utility bills (water, sewage, electricity, phone, etc.), and any other special characteristic, limitation, or encumbrance pertaining to the property.

The investor must enter into the Promise to Purchase Agreement, which allows time to complete the above due diligence. For titled properties, this agreement is recorded in the Public Registry Office. After due diligence has been completed, the investor enters into the Purchase and Sale Agreement, which includes an indemnification clause to protect against hidden defects of the property.

The buyer does not pay the seller until ownership of the land is properly transferred. In an alternative arrangement, the parties can agree to appoint an escrow agent (usually a lawyer or banker) who receives the funds under an escrow agreement. The agreement states that payment will be made upon presentation of the deed of transfer of ownership of the property, duly recorded at the Public Registry Office. Title insurance should be considered for the full price of the property. Generally, title insurance is well received in Panama because it provides assurance of investment in both land and improvements.

Things to Know

The following are some things to be aware of if you are purchasing property as a nonresident.

Commissions. Realtor commissions are usually 5 percent of the selling price, although this varies depending on the location. They are typically paid by the seller. The buyer must pay the expenses, including the registration of title and lawyers' fees. The amount to be paid is prescribed in the Fiscal Code.

Title insurance. Title insurance may protect against most problems connected to errors and fraud. It is available in Panama only through CONASE, a prestigious local insurance company that is fully supported and reinsured in Panama through LandAmerica Lawyers Title Insurance Corporation.

Transfer taxes. The seller must pay a 2 percent transfer tax when the property is transferred if the seller has owned the property for less than twenty-four months. The 2 percent amount is based on the higher of two values: the sale price stated in the Purchase and Sale Agreement or the official property value. If the seller has owned the property for more than twenty-four months, the seller can choose to pay income tax at a fixed 10 percent rate, without having to add the sale price to taxable income and deduct the property transfer tax already paid. The Public Registry Office requires a tax clearance certificate before any real estate transaction can be officially recorded.

Mortgages. Generally, financing is available for 60–70 percent of the purchase price or appraised market value, whichever is less. The maximum amortization is twenty years, beginning with a five-year term that is renewable at the bank's option for three additional terms of five years each. The maximum amortization is typically subject to such factors as the borrower's age and net worth. Security for the loan is the first mortgage over the property. Banks usually require the borrower to contract a life insurance policy for the amount of the loan, endorsed to the bank, and a fire insurance policy with catastrophic extension for the amount of the loan, also endorsed to the bank. Such insurance must be underwritten in Panama.

The bank's commission is about 1 percent of the loan amount, payable at the time of the loan drawdown. The borrower must also pay all legal and registration expenses charged by the bank; provide an appraisal to show that the estimated market value is at least equal to the purchase price; open a savings account at the bank through which loan payments will be deducted, with a minimum balance equal to three monthly installments; and meet with the bank's lending officer at least once.

Banks typically require the following documentation: copy of the purchase agreement; two clear copies of ID cards or all passport pages; copies of the last three personal income tax declarations and/or business income tax declarations or audited financial statements; adequate verification of sufficient personal assets (copies of bank statements, real estate titles, common stock, bonds, and so on); job letter and copy of two pay slips (for borrowers currently getting a salary); and credit references.

Potential irregularities. The notary is responsible for verifying the identity of the seller and buyer. If a forgery or impersonation occurs, the transfer is null and void, and the registration is amended accordingly. If duress or fraud are involved, leading to an absence of actual consent, the transaction could be reversed by judicial declaration. If there are suspected irregularities in the original title document (that is, the public deed through which the seller secured title), an investigation should take place at the Public Registry Office to look for errors in such matters as the identity of the owner, the price, the description of property, and so on. If a document related to the transaction, such as power of attorney, is invalid, the transaction is voided.

The registrar is entrusted with ensuring that the measurements and areas of the property in the agreement match those in the Public Registry. If there are incomplete or inaccurate measurements, the buyer can demand an abatement of the purchase price if the size is smaller. However, if the size is bigger, the buyer is obligated to supplement the original price. Because these obligations usually have to be judicially enforced, it is customary in cases where the property has irregular measurements to conduct a survey.

Generally, an error that finds its way into the Public Registry can be corrected by a notary's filing. An error made by the registrar can be corrected by the registrar unilaterally or upon request of the interested party, and processing fees are waived. The applicant pays the fees if the applicant is the source of the error. If the notary is responsible for the error, the notary is subject to liability.

Capital gains taxes. Capital gains are taxed in full and on a separate basis regardless of whether the individual had a net income or a net operating loss. If the seller chooses to pay income tax according to the applicable rate, the transfer tax can be offset as a direct credit against the income tax levied on a capital gain arising from the sale. If the seller chooses to pay income tax at a flat 10 percent rate, no further taxes on capital gains are levied, but the seller cannot apply that 10 percent rate to the sums already paid for the property transfer tax and any expenses related to the transaction. Sale of a new residential property is exempt from this tax if the buyer uses it as a personal residency.

Property tax. All real estate improvements are subject to property tax, which is appraised by a government agency. It must be paid according to the official assessment value, which is usually the declared value on the sale document. The tax varies depending on the value of the property. Property tax has priority over all encumbrances on the property. It typically is paid in three installments, at the end of April, August, and December.

New Zealand: The Right Place at the Right Time

Every so often a pop culture event expands into a phenomenon, bringing with it a dramatic upsurge of interest in people or places not used to such attention. When the trilogy of movies based on J. R. R. Tolkien's *Lord of the Rings* dominated theaters and DVD players, not to mention the Academy Awards, a lot of viewers had the same question: Where did they find that beautiful countryside?

Barbara didn't have to ask that question. More than once she had vacationed in New Zealand with her physicist husband, Pat, and they both loved the country. But on her current visit to Auckland, the country's principal port on North Island, she has her eye on more than the gorgeous landscapes. That's what thirty years of experience in commercial and residential real estate in the United States and abroad will do to someone.

Barbara's extensive experience in the U.S. and international property markets has taught her about dealing with inefficient, even hostile bureaucracies and about weathering real estate slumps and currency fluctuations. Over the years she has developed an uncanny ability to size up opportunities rapidly, both to take advantage of good deals and to know when to avoid deals that are too good to be

71

true. She also has studied the effect of international monetary mechanisms on real estate investment by nonresidents. And because she's smart enough to realize she can't know everything, she hires capable legal counsel and accountants who are versed in the intricacies of international transactions.

Assessing the Market

Barbara evolves an investment strategy for her foray into New Zealand real estate. Her primary goal is to make property deals when the exchange rates are with her. She will not repatriate cash when the exchange rates are against her, and she will leave income cash in the country, unless she needs to hedge against loss. At the time of Barbara's purchase, the New Zealand dollar is a bargain compared to the U.S. dollar and European currencies, making properties much less expensive.

With regard to the real estate itself, she plans to read up carefully on properties that are going to be auctioned. Selling properties at auction is becoming more popular in New Zealand. These are usually properties whose value isn't easily determined, such as a unique luxury property or one that requires major renovation. Repossessed properties are also sold at auction. Barbara is familiar with buying auctioned properties and knows how to size up their value. She has discovered during her three decades of experience that many people fail to read addenda to the property deeds, which can provide invaluable clues. Once, thanks to her extra reading, she was able to purchase a property that had been undervalued by a ten-to-one ratio, because the auction description hadn't adequately represented the land up for sale. She is also prepared to pay the required 10 percent deposit if her bid is successful.

But before she takes the plunge, Barbara is aware that she must step back from the small details of currency exchange rates and property deeds to take a much broader view. In other words, she looks at the overall state of the investing environment in New Zealand with regard to nonresidents. First and foremost, she learns that the New Zealand government, through its administrative arm, the Overseas Investment Office, has no major issues against overseas property investors. In fact, because of the growing population, foreign investment actually is helping to meet new housing demands.

She also determines that property prices in New Zealand are relatively inexpensive when compared with property in other first-world countries. Added to that, New Zealand does not have a property purchase tax, land tax, capital gains tax, stamp duty, or mortgage stamp duty. Another tax advantage is the comparatively high depreciation rate of 4 percent per annum on buildings, regardless of their age, beginning at the date of purchase. This is more tax friendly than depreciation rates in, for example, the United States or in Australia, New Zealand's nearest major neighbor.

Some general demographic trends in New Zealand are encouraging to Barbara as she prepares to enter the rental market. Most New Zealanders tend to be tenants before they are owners, and there has been an increasing trend in the country toward later marriage, meaning that people often rent for longer periods. Some cities are experiencing an influx of foreign students, and New Zealand in general has been experiencing "positive migration," which is a fancy way of saying more population, and therefore more overall rental demand.

The most popular real estate venue for investment is residential property. Among desirable areas are Auckland, where Barbara is staying; the Bay of Islands region; and the holiday resort areas in the Central Otago and Lakes districts on South Island, around the city of Queenstown. Queenstown ranks as one of the top locations for both local and international property investment, due to its fame as a holiday destination for tourists worldwide, so Barbara decides to focus her real estate savvy on Auckland, where she may find better deals and less competition for them.

Diving In

Barbara doesn't waste any time, to say the least. Within two days she identifies six single-family dwellings in Auckland, determines that they will bring in her desired net operating income (NOI) of 6 percent, and buys them all, and she has all of them rented out in one month. She may be able to move with incredible alacrity, but let's slow her down for our purposes and see what she does, why she does it, and how she knows it's the right thing to do.

Barbara wants to do the purchases using borrowed funds. She is introduced to two New Zealand lenders through her banker contacts in the United States. She learns that the banks want proof of identity to open an account, charge an appraisal fee of about NZ$300 to NZ$500, and charge an equivalent inspector's fee. Some also charge an application fee. She also discovers that she can easily refinance properties if she wants to free up money to buy other properties. With equity from another property, the banks will finance up to 80 percent loan to value, and at no charge.

The first bank requires a provable financial statement, and it requires proof of income if Barbara puts 30 percent down. The second bank calls for the same type of financial statement, and in addition it asks for Barbara's income tax returns from the previous three years. However, in light of the complexity of obtaining those returns, the bank waives its requirement. And so in a matter of a few hours, Barbara has two lenders ready and willing to make investment property loans to her. She chooses the second bank, which establishes a business account for her so she can purchase the multiple properties with a single loan.

The loan is an adjustable rate mortgage fixed for three years. There will be no cost for rolling over the mortgage for another two- to three-year term. The rate is 8 percent, at a time when the similar rate for a fully amortizing loan in the United States is 5 percent. Barbara arranges to wire U.S. dollars to her Auckland account. The

Auckland bank does not charge any incoming wire fees. As a U.S. taxpayer, she must file a W-9 at the bank.

Barbara has researched the following basic details of a purchase in New Zealand and has found it to be very similar to the process in the United States. Most buyers and sellers use realtors. Commissions run about 4 percent of the purchase price and are paid by the seller. Once a written contract is accepted, a 10 percent down payment is typically expected. The closing date is negotiated, and a solicitor and attorney usually are part of the closing. The buyer pays the attorney's fee, which runs about NZ$800 to NZ$1,200. There are nominal registration fees, and closing costs are virtually nil.

New Zealand follows English common law. An attorney checks to ensure clear title, but title insurance is not required. The attorney also provides the Land Information Memorandum, which reports everything that is known about the property, such as additions and modifications, potential hazards, and past and present liens (at a cost of about NZ$350). Barbara arranges to provide the appropriate insurance that is required by the lender.

New Zealand does not have a land tax or stamp tax. If the rental property is sold as a going concern in a business operation, the government would impose the Government Sales Tax (GST), which the buyer pays unless otherwise negotiated, but this is not a factor in Barbara's single-family-dwelling properties.

New Zealand does impose a rates tax, however, that Barbara will need to pay. New Zealand city and district councils assess properties within their areas to levy rates for funding local services such as roads, sewers and drainage systems, libraries, and so on. Every property in New Zealand must be assessed at least once every three years.

The typical charge for managing properties in New Zealand is about 7–8 percent. Many real estate agencies offer such services. Barbara hires a property manager to oversee all six of her properties. She learns that rental agreements are the same throughout New Zealand, and the renter posts a bond. Rent payments are usually made weekly and by direct deposit. If the tenant fails to pay the rent, the bond is forfeited to the property owner and the tenant is evicted relatively quickly.

She decides to have the income automatically credited to her bank account in New Zealand on a net basis, and asks the property manager to be in charge of filing her New Zealand tax returns. Barbara's U.S. accountant receives statements from her New Zealand bank and property manager to complete her U.S. income tax returns, because she is taxed in the United States on her worldwide income. However, she plans to take advantage of the U.S. tax laws that allow for the application of tax credits against taxes paid in foreign jurisdictions.

Looking to the Future

Barbara is indeed a savvy investor. Barbara's venture into the New Zealand real estate market took place in 2001 when the economy wasn't quite as bustling as today, and the New Zealand dollar was worth 40 cents in the United States. Today, it's closer to 70 cents—so Barbara's experience is a classic example of being in the right place at the right time. The increased strength in the New Zealand dollar has also affected the economy. Property values to rents received have changed considerably, and some say that the real estate investor market has reached its top. Property values in New Zealand experienced 6 percent annual growth from September 2005 to October 2006. During that same period, Auckland's median home price rose from NZ$220,000 to NZ$260,000. Auckland's property value growth has remained strong and at or around the national average. Barbara's properties have obviously gained in value, and it is to her advantage to keep her funds in New Zealand, although she will continue to monitor the currency rate against the U.S. dollar and euro so that she can keep apprised of the desirability of investing in New Zealand versus Europe and other parts of the world. For now, Barbara plans future investment in New Zealand as long as her NOI is at least 6 percent.

She also knows the importance of staying abreast of the political and economic climate. She's aware that in 2007 the government is considering legislation regarding transferring large tracts of land to the Maori, the indigenous people of New Zealand. This could potentially involve reverting land that is currently developed and occupied, in which case, the current occupant must settle with the tribe. The settlement could take the form of a leasehold or repurchasing the properties.

C H A P T E R

Vacation Time in Austria

When Walter decided to look at real estate investments overseas, it was natural that his first choice would be Austria, a country in which he has family and whose language he is familiar with. Once he had set his sights on Austria, his next step was natural as well—looking at property in Innsbruck, near his favorite ski resort. Nestled in the Tyrolean Alps, Innsbruck is the famed site of the 1964 and 1976 Winter Olympics as well as a popular destination both locally and internationally for mountaineering in the summer and skiing in the winter. His plan was to buy a property that he could rent out to tourists who wanted to spend stretches of time exploring the city and the many picturesque villages and sights nearby and that he could reserve for himself when he wished.

Before investigating the ins and outs of how Walter obtained his property, let's cut to the chase: Austrian real estate is among the most expensive in Europe. In addition, the cost of living in Austria is generally higher than any other country in Europe. In investor surveys and international rankings, Austria consistently earns high marks for quality of life, personal security, rule of law, the skill and motivation of the work force, and the strength of its health-care system. However, it receives low marks for the tax burden, regulatory red tape, rigid labor practices, restrictive immigration laws, and the size of the public sector.

Politically and economically, the country is stable. In 2003, Austria experienced two large strikes in response to government pension and railroad reform initiatives. Most observers characterized these strikes as political actions against the government rather than management-labor disputes and noted that they had limited and only transitory economic impact. Since then, Austria has remained virtually strike free, even with the continued implementation of the government's reform agenda, including contentious issues such as the harmonization of different pension systems.

Despite the high costs, nonresidents are enjoying positive cash flow from properties used as vacation or seasonal rentals. This, coupled with the tax benefits that occur when a property is held long term, has made investing in Austria attractive. Real estate that is used as a primary residence or is held for more than ten years is exempt from capital gains tax. Otherwise, capital gains on the sale of real estate is taxed as regular income at 34 percent.

Nonresidents tend to buy second homes or vacation property. There are virtually no restrictions on foreign investment in Austria, and foreign investors for the most part receive the same treatment as Austrian nationals. Historically, Germans are the largest group of foreigners purchasing investment real estate in Austria. And in recent years, the government has taken significant steps to streamline and simplify the manner in which nonresidents can invest in real estate, especially those from the European Union (EU). When it comes to foreigners from non-EU nations purchasing real estate, the investor must obtain permission from the local authority office, which is easily and quickly granted in the vast majority of cases.

Buying a Place in Town

Walter was familiar with Austrian politics and didn't see much in the way of affecting the value of his purchase in the immediate future. He was concerned about the growing devastation of the nearby forests caused by acid rain, but he knew that the problems were not isolated to the area but were far more global. If anything were to happen, the Austrian legal system would be effective at protecting the property and contractual rights of nonresidents. Expropriation of private property in Austria is rare and when it occurs, the owner must receive just compensation. The government can instigate expropriation only if it is exclusively in the public interest and no other alternative exists for satisfying the public interest. The expropriation process is fully transparent and nondiscriminatory toward nonresidents.

As Walter began moving forward on his purchase, he briefly considered building on unimproved land outside Innsbruck, but he decided against it once he determined that the permit process was unusually long for his purposes. Also, he would have to make payments according to district regulations, which would require him to cover the costs and expenses related to preparing the land for building and providing for service connections, which could prove extensive, especially in the more rural areas.

Once he chose to limit his options to already existing properties in the city of Innsbruck itself, Walter researched the prospect of obtaining a mortgage. On top of requiring a 50 percent down payment, the cost of a mortgage involved the following fees:

- Mortgage arrangement fee: 0.8 percent
- General order of precedence for the mortgage: 0.6 percent
- Cost for drawing up the mortgage offer: according to the fee scale of the respective conveyancer
- Searches and stamp duties: according to published schedules
- Appraisals or valuations (if required): according to the professional scale of fees
- Commission not to exceed 2 percent of the loan amount (although under certain circumstances the commission could go as high as 5 percent)

Walter found that as a nonresident it was no problem getting financing from an Austrian bank. However, in light of the high cost of obtaining a mortgage, Walter chose to make an all-cash transaction for a place in town. The euro is the only legal tender in Austria, so he needed to take the exchange rates into account. There are no restrictions in Austria on converting or transferring funds associated with a foreign investment.

Wunderbar, Walter found his ideal property—one he felt would be easy to rent on an occasional basis and provide a place away from home when he wanted to hit the slopes. As per Austrian protocol, he made a verbal offer to the seller. The seller made a counteroffer that was agreeable to Walter, so the next step was to draw up a purchase agreement with the help of a lawyer proficient in handling real estate.

Typically, the buyer posts a 10 percent deposit at the time the purchase agreement is executed. The deposit is held in escrow, pending the completion of the transaction. If the sale falls apart through no fault of the buyer, the deposit is returned. Prior to closing, the seller is responsible for satisfying all applicable contract provisions—primarily ensuring that the property is free from any encumbrances that might impede the conveyance of the real estate to the buyer.

At closing, Walter needs to have his financing in place and pay the remaining balance due, including the 3.5 percent transfer tax and the deed registry fee of 1 percent. Because of Austria's historic bureaucratic rules, registering the real estate with the Austrian Land Registry can take up to three or four months in some instances.

Buyer's Remorse

A few years have gone by, and Walter realizes that he hasn't used the property as often as he thought he would, as he lives too far away to travel there easily. He can't decide whether he regrets the decision, but he knows he has to do something with his property. On his next visit, he investigates his options: selling it or renting it out on a long-term basis.

Walter consults with Wolfgang, his local financial tax advisor, about the implications of selling. Wolfgang informs him that he would need to pay a capital gains tax of 34 percent, because he's had the property for less than ten years. The process of the sale would be simple; overall, the transaction would be no more complicated than the purchase of the property. One catch, though: if Walter uses an agent, he must pay a commission to the agent whether or not the property sells, unless he can negotiate otherwise.

Renting the property is a little more complex for Walter than merely advertising in the local *Tiroler Tageszeitung*. Not only are there fees and commissions involved, but also he must keep in mind that the rent cannot be freely negotiated—Austria has landlord-tenant laws that regulate the amount of rent that can be charged. In addition, he must pay a rental contract arrangement fee of 1 percent of the gross rent, including a value-added tax due for the duration of the contract, to a maximum of eighteen times the net annual value. For an open-ended rental contract, the fee is 1 percent of three times the net annual value. If the rental agreement is for a fixed term, and the property is predominantly used for residential purposes, fees for arranging the contract are limited to three times the net annual value. There are also the standard fees for drawing up the rental contract, which is usually done by agreement between the parties and within the fee scale of the respective conveyors.

Net rental income earned by a foreign corporation is taxable in Austria at the rate of 25 percent, which is the corporate income tax rate. The income tax rates for individuals range from 0 percent on the first €3,640 of taxable income, and then 21 percent for the next €3,630 of taxable income, to 50 percent on income in excess of €50,870. Rental income is based on income minus expenses. The following major categories of deductions are permitted: maintenance and repairs, property management and administration, financing costs and interest payments, insurance premiums, depreciation, and real estate tax.

Austria and the United States are parties to a bilateral double-taxation treaty covering income and corporate taxes, which went into effect on February 1, 1998. An additional bilateral double-taxation treaty covering estates, inheritances, gifts, and generation-skipping transfers has been in effect since 1982.

Walter is a bit overwhelmed by it all. He contacts his Austrian cousin Bruno, who is an agent. If Bruno sells or rents the property to a family member, or to someone with whom he has a financially close relationship, he can only claim a commission from Walter if he immediately informs Walter of the relationship. Furthermore, the commission can only be paid if the transaction is consummated; in other words, Bruno may not claim an advance.

Walter can also enter into an agreement with Bruno whereby he pays Bruno for expenses and effort, and then pays a commission based on an agreed-upon or typical local commission should Bruno successfully sell or rent the property. Problems could arise between Walter and Bruno if any of the following occurred: (1) the transaction that Bruno arranges as per their contract fails to take place because Walter, without good reason, doesn't provide the required legal instruments; (2) Bruno negotiates a transaction that is different from the transaction authorized within the scope of the Walter-Bruno agreement; (3) the transaction does not take place with the negotiated third party but with another party made aware of the opportunity through that third party; or (4) the transaction does not take place with the negotiated third party.

Poor Walter. Maybe he should have looked at property in Aspen. What keeps him optimistic, though, is that the property is desirable and he can pass it on to his children, who have inherited his love of skiing. By the way, the estate taxes match the steepness of the slopes, ranging from 2 percent to 60 percent, depending on the value of the property and inheritance status.

10

Morocco: An Affordable Mediterranean Climate

Most people are surprised to learn that the oldest official relationship of the United States is with Morocco. Back in 1777, the fledgling republic started to send out merchant ships across the Atlantic, but they often came under attack by the infamous pirates who menaced the Barbary Coast of North Africa. The newly founded United States tried futilely to enlist the help of European powers, but it was Sultan Sidi Mohamed of Morocco who declared that American merchant ships thereafter sailed under his sultanate's protection. The Moroccan-American Treaty of Friendship, signed by John Adams and Thomas Jefferson on this side of the ocean in 1786, represents the oldest unbroken friendship treaty of the United States. The consulate in Tangier holds the distinction of being the first property the American government ever owned abroad.

Our interest, of course, is in present-day Morocco. The Morocco of today has one of the fastest-growing real estate markets in Africa for foreign investment. Politically, the country has enjoyed relative stability. Since declaring its independence from France in 1956, Morocco has been ruled by a constitutional monarch. The king enjoys vast executive powers, but there also is an elected parliament. It remains the only country on the continent that is not a part of the African Union. Financially, Morocco has the fifth-strongest economy in Africa (as measured by gross domestic product). With its temperate Mediterranean climate, famous cuisine, busy outdoor markets, and historical architecture in the old city areas, Morocco has evolved into a powerful tourist draw. It has been a popular refuge for artists and writers, and many Europeans go there to spend a relaxing weekend in a *riad*—a luxurious house built around a patio garden.

All this attracted Peggy, who went to Morocco as a tourist and found it so compelling that she decided to find a way to return again, again, and again. But before we look into how Peggy found a way to get a piece of Morocco, let's explore some of the general features of the Moroccan real estate market.

A Sound, Fast-Growing Market

Foreign investment in Moroccan real estate has proven to reap sound and solid rewards. The value of property has increased steadily over time, and there are minimal tax implications on property held for a certain amount of time. Of nearly equal importance, the market has avoided overheating, a phenomenon that mars many other countries, because it is usually followed by a collapse to some degree.

In an attempt to increase capital investment in Morocco, the government has been streamlining the process for nonresidents to buy real estate. Since 2000, the government has also instituted a formal policy of promoting tourism. As a result of these two factors, many foreigners are buying real estate for vacation purposes in different regions of the country, both for personal use and for leasing or renting to other vacationers.

Morocco is an ethnically diverse country. Today, most Moroccans are Sunni Muslims. Arabic is the country's official language, but French remains the unofficial second language left over from the time when Morocco was a protectorate of France. French is still taught throughout the country and continues to serve as Morocco's primary language of commerce and economics. English, however, is becoming the foreign language of choice among Morocco's educated youth. As a result of national education reforms in 2002, English is now taught in all public schools after the fourth year.

Nonresidents hold all types of real estate in the country: commercial, industrial, and residential. With regard to residential real estate, which is the main focus here, the majority of nonresident real estate is owned by French nationals, due to the status of Morocco as a protectorate of France in the first half of the twentieth century. The market in apartments in commercial centers of Morocco has been brisk since 2000. Some foreign nationals invest in these apartments to use as long-term residences for business purposes, whereas others lease or rent them to other nonresidents, particularly tourists. Again, this investment has been led by the French, but other nonresidents have recently been venturing into the country as well, attracted by the favorable business and vacation climates.

Agents are essential for real estate transactions in Morocco. Although verbal offers are made, the agent documents the buyer's offer. If the seller accepts, a preliminary contract is drafted by an attorney, who typically uses standard forms. When the preliminary contract is executed, the buyer places a refundable deposit of 10 percent to 30 percent, usually due within thirty days of the preliminary contract. The balance of payment is due upon signing the final agreement.

Non-Moroccans are required to establish bank accounts in Morocco to complete the purchase. The account must be in place on or before the final agreement is executed. Financing is generally available with a 30 percent down payment, with interest on a fixed basis, which was close to 7 percent at the end of 2006.

The seller is responsible for providing clear title to the buyer, which usually takes about two to three months. Once the final agreement is signed and full payment is made, the registration process takes a matter of days, after which the buyer becomes the owner of the property.

The Richness of a Riad

My friend Peggy has been very successful in the Victorian rehab business in California for over twenty years, and she has converted many of those homes into income properties. She uses property managers for all of her properties, and she has an excellent accountant who keeps her up to date on her financial health and ensures that all required reporting is properly completed.

In addition to loving Victorians, Peggy loves Morocco, especially Marrakech. Marrakech is a vibrant city with much historical and cultural significance. It has the largest traditional market (*souk*) in Morocco and what many consider the busiest and most dazzling square in all of Africa, *Djemaa el Fna*. Peggy has been visiting the city, particularly the *medina* (or old city), as many as six times a year, and now she has decided to put her real estate investment acumen to work in her adopted second country.

Peggy learns that any investment income she makes in Morocco is not subject to income tax there. Further, there is little significant local tax in Marrakech—perhaps a few hundred dollars for municipal services. If she sells a property within five years, the capital gains tax is 20 percent, but if she sells the property after holding it for five years or more, she pays no capital gains or any other related tax.

Peggy's first step is to employ French-speaking Hassan, a real estate agent who has been recommended to her by people she trusts. She asks Hassan to be on the lookout for riads, which are large residences characterized by one or several inner courtyards graced by fountains, flowering vines, and fruit trees. They usually have large living rooms, bedrooms, and bathrooms, and often have steam rooms and swimming pools. In addition to their size and elegance, riads also are amazingly quiet, even when located in the busier sections of the city, thanks to the architectural concept that centers every room around the inner courtyards. Because of their luxury and peacefulness, they are popular destinations for tourists and visitors to the area.

Apparently word has gotten out that an American with substantial investment potential is interested in the Marrakech market. Peggy is approached by Francois, a Frenchman who acquired his riad in 1986. He has clear title to the property, but he suggests to Peggy that he would prefer to have the funds from the purchase sent to an account he maintains in another country. In Morocco, funding transactions properly is imperative, and Peggy's attorney strongly weighs in against doing the deal with Francois, who may be engaged in a tax-avoidance scheme. Although it's a great deal, Peggy declines Francois's offer, deciding it's not worth the risk.

Her disappointment in turning down the riad is short-lived when Hassan shows Peggy a beauty. This 300-year-old riad is more than 4,000 square feet, located in Marrakech's *medina*. It is divided into two large suites, one with a swimming pool. The rooms are sumptuous, the bathrooms spacious. There is a beautiful courtyard in the center of the riad, and each suite also has its own courtyard. An expansive dining room can accommodate guests from both suites, and there is a kitchen in which to prepare delicious meals in the famed Moroccan cuisine.

Peggy decides to buy not only the riad but also the corporation that owns it for approximately $1 million. The riad of course is attractive on its merits, but the corporation is attractive for how it can help her in the future, because she gains its clients who have stayed at the riad and its contracts for services with third-party providers, such as property management and accounting. Peggy is able to secure a 7 percent loan on a fixed term by making a 30 percent down payment with a local bank.

Most of Peggy's guests at the riad are European. For example, a Londoner can make the three-hour flight to Marrakech for about €200 and rent one of the suites with a private pool for €500 a night, which includes food and transport to and from the airport by a private driver. The riad is fully booked except for a few weeks in July and August, the hottest time of the year in Marrakech. The gross on the property promises to be about $725,000 annually.

So Peggy now has a very healthy cash-flowing property. She must add this net income to her worldwide income for U.S. tax purposes, but she doesn't have to be concerned about Morocco at all—neither Morocco nor Marrakech will tax any of her net income. Not surprisingly, Peggy is looking for other Marrakech properties. She has her sights on four other riads in the *medina*, confident that she will have no problem converting them into cash-flowing properties as well.

The demand for riad living continues to increase, and the Moroccan government continues to be supportive of foreign investment. Having learned from her property experience in California, she plans to operate these future purchases through local Marrakech property management companies and to use her corporation as a source of dependable employees, such as cooks, maintenance staff, drivers, and concierges. Also drawing on her Victorian rehab background, she empowers her property management representatives to continually apprise her of any maintenance needs, so she can retain and improve on over 300 years of craftsmanship.

11

Offshore Real Estate Checklist

Terms such as "global economy" and "global markets" are used freely these days—perhaps too freely. Yes, the technological tidal wave of the Internet has swept spectacularly through even the world's most underdeveloped nations, providing a worldwide electronic connectedness of information and exchange. But the wise offshore investor must also keep in mind that powerful computers, ubiquitous cell phones, and smart little PDAs can provide a false sense of unity and control. Countries are still separated by such fundamental differences as language, customs, currency, border disputes, religious beliefs, unresolved historical issues, and a myriad of lesser but still troublesome complexities. In light of the underlying variations from one country to the next, the cautious offshore investor must first consider the "Big Questions."

The Big Questions

☐ Are there internal issues—such as civil unrest, a repressive government, a history of military intervention in political matters, an upsurge in religious fundamentalism, racial hostilities, pervasive distrust of foreigners—that may make the country unstable in your lifetime or in the lifetime of those whom you may hope to someday benefit from your investments?

☐ Are there corruption issues—national or regional government corruption or failure to prosecute those engaged in nefarious business dealings? Did you consult Transparency International's corruption perception index (www.transparency.org) to get up-to-date information?

☐ Are there external issues—such as border problems with neighboring countries, influxes of immigrants or refugees, overt or covert threats of terrorism—that may make the country unstable?

☐ Are there foreseeable ecological concerns—pollution, deforestation, overfarming, water and/or food shortages, not to mention the increasing anxiety about the possible effects of global warming, particularly on coastal areas—that may make the country's economic future less desirable?

☐ Are there societal and cultural changes—religious or tribal strife, large immigrant populations, increasing disparity between rich and poor, underfunded or collapsing educational systems—that may make the stability of the country's overall future less predictable?

If you checked any of the above boxes with regard to a country you have been considering for a real estate investment, you should carefully reconsider. Clearly, you have more research to do.

Fundamental Money Matters

Once past the Big Questions, you still have fundamental money matters to ponder, because investment is, after all, about money. Whereas in the checklist above, a checked box indicates you need to reconsider your investment choice, in the following list the more boxes you check, the closer you are to making an intelligent investment decision.

- [ ] Have you verified that you possess, or can gain access to, the money you need to fund your offshore real estate venture?
- [ ] Is the money you have earmarked for this investment disposable?
- [ ] Are you able to withstand losing any or all of the capital you intend to invest?
- [ ] Have you established a reasonable goal with regard to the return you expect from your investment after expenses?
- [ ] Have you carefully researched the tax implications of your investment, both in the country you want to invest in as well as in your home country?
- [ ] Have you determined whether there are relevant tax treaties between your home country and the country you want to invest in, and if so, how such treaties will impact you?
- [ ] Have you adequately established the proper legal channels through which money must be moved to the country?
- [ ] Have you investigated the historic currency risk between your source of money and the money used in your country of investment?
- [ ] Have you considered the effect of inflation on any of the currencies that will be in play for your transaction?

The Transaction Details

Once you feel you've chosen the right country and that you understand the potential implications of an offshore investment to your financial health and well-being, it's time to get down to the nitty-gritty of what a foreign real estate transaction entails. Use the following four-part checklist as a helpful guide with regard to your desired country of investment.

Initial Decision Making

- ☐ Determine any limitation on foreign investment in real estate, including whether governmental authorities can expropriate property.
- ☐ Decide on the type of property—residential, commercial, or agricultural.
- ☐ Decide on the use of the property—investment, vacation, residency, or a combination of uses.
- ☐ Decide on how the property is best acquired—personally or through a corporation, trust, or foundation.
- ☐ Research the legal aspects of ownership and any issues regarding rights of survivorship and estate taxes.
- ☐ Set a realistic timetable for the transaction.
- ☐ Consider who will need to be involved—agents, attorneys, notaries, accountants, local officials.

Property Issues

- ☐ Determine whether the property has any title-related issues— unclear title, encumbrances (easements, rights-of-way, mortgages, taxes), or outstanding third-party litigation or claims.
- ☐ Examine, or hire an expert to examine, the property itself and any relevant property documents, topographical maps, and surveys.
- ☐ Research the potential effects of governmental requirements, related cultural exclusions or inclusions, zoning and design ordinances, building regulations and codes, homeowners association rules, and any necessary permits and restrictions with regard to improvements.
- ☐ Determine whether tenants or others might have preemption rights that may deter the sale.
- ☐ Consider environmental issues, such as existing contamination and hazardous waste problems; air, water, and noise pollution; and the condition and reliability of social services, such as utilities, roads, police and fire departments, and medical facilities.

Contractual Issues

☐ Establish the necessity, and extent of participation, of the various parties, such as agents, brokers, bankers, legal counsel, government officials, and so on.

☐ Determine that the seller can legally dispose of the property and whether there are any restrictions on transferability.

☐ Determine whether there are any outstanding agreements (lease, rental) or prior real estate tax issues.

☐ Investigate which types of identification you and/or your corporation, trust, foundation, and others need.

☐ Determine which types of agreements, including any preliminary agreements, need to be written up and signed and by whom.

☐ Understand any relevant timetable restrictions with regard to due diligence, rescission, tenant issues, insurance, funding, and so on.

☐ Research the nature of contract law in the country and how it may differ from contract law in your home country.

☐ Conduct any required due diligence.

☐ Check whether you need to acquire, or can acquire, any necessary insurance, such as title, earthquake, flood, and so on.

☐ Understand how registration of ownership is finalized.

Financial Issues

☐ Establish the method of funding the transaction, for instance, how the money will be brought into the country and how it will be applied to the purchase.

☐ Determine what the broker/agent commissions and fees are and who is responsible for paying them: the seller and/or buyer.

☐ Calculate the extent of all transaction-related expenses, such as booking deposits, attorneys' fees, surveys, engineering reports, hazard inspections, registration fees, stamp duties, and auctioneers' fees.

☐ Determine which taxes are involved—transfer, real estate, income, capital gains, estate—and how they are assessed in the country of your investment and your home country.

☐ Research the desirability of a debt-financed purchase and the proper steps that must be taken if a mortgage is chosen instead of an all-cash transaction. Determine whether you need to assign power of attorney to an agent or other person to finalize any paperwork if you are unable to stay in the country.

☐ Find someone local to handle property management and other upkeep matters.

Scams

There's a scam born every minute, and unfortunately, a fool to go with it. We, the public, as well as professionals, are constantly subjected to information that is intended to convince us to buy real estate and debt instruments (such as mortgage loans) offshore. Determining which ones are legitimate and which ones are scams is not always easy. The proliferation of the Internet has also helped scams breed faster. You may think the website is nice, so the deal's got to be legitimate. The location, the price, the ease: the package is all so enticing. Two words: due diligence. Whenever you are considering a new prospect, perform your due diligence. If you cannot get your questions answered to your satisfaction, it may be best to move on. Working with knowledgeable professionals you trust is helpful in weeding out the scams from the good deals. If you know locals who are familiar with the market and how things are done, talk to them. Gather as much information as you can.

But He Seemed So Nice

Some scams are obvious to detect; others are more subtle. The subtle scams are those in which the seller is misrepresenting or overrepresenting a property. For instance, a property may have no cash flow, tenant problems, or a defect such as electrical or plumbing issues that are too expensive to repair. Disclosure requirements vary from country to country, and most countries don't have sophisticated disclosure rules or laws, so it's buyer beware. The best way to see through the subtle scams is to do your own due diligence. To investigate a purported cash flow, get information such as rental rates for the area and type of property, vacancy rates, upkeep costs, taxes, and fees from independent third parties. The more you know about the local economy, the better.

An example of a subtle scam recently occurred on a Caribbean island that had been ravaged by a hurricane. Much of the housing had been destroyed, so a lot of new construction was taking place. One of the builders was constructing apartments that could be converted to condominiums. The prospect of having new construction with immediate cash flow as a rental as well as the potential of converting it to a sellable condo can seem quite appealing. The builder gave optimistic information regarding rental income, tax incentives, and occupancy rates. Because the island was a popular destination, the builder made highly optimistic and convincing claims regarding appreciation. However, on closer examination, it turned out that the builder had overbuilt and had a tremendous cash flow problem. Rather than take a loss, the builder inflated the numbers, hoping to sell some of the property to recover his money. Many unwary people bought—and continue to buy—these properties. If those who had bought had looked into it, they would have discovered that people were in fact not moving into the area, and apartments were remaining unoccupied for months. Rents were about 30 percent below what was touted, and appreciation was a long way off. By doing due diligence, it was easy to discover that other builders who had hoped to provide good opportunities to renters and investors had also fallen on hard times. Some builders would not recover their investment for many years. What started out as a problem for the builder, turned into puffery and subtle scamming of the public and even other investors.

It Sounded Like a Good Deal

Not so subtle scams involve the perpetrator knowing that the foreign investor may be unprepared to learn and comprehend local real estate matters. Language differences often work to the advantage of the scam artist. Many foreign investors make the mistake of thinking that purchasing property in another country works the same way as in their home country. There is a big difference between same and similar. Watch out for the scam artist who attempts to convince you otherwise or tries to minimize the differences as being insignificant. This is not an issue that only happens in emerging third-world countries; it occurs in first-world countries as well. One of the most common scams is to sell you a property that the "seller" doesn't own, such as in our example in Panama. It's always important to do a title search and make sure that the legitimate owner is selling the property. Of course, such examples are not limited to other countries; they also occur daily in the United States.

Overbuying is another popular scam. This involves purchasing income property for more than it is worth. The seller convinces you that the beachfront property in an equatorial country is such a good deal that the seller will guarantee the advertised income on it for the first year after your purchase. The $250,000 sales price sounds like a bargain to you, compared with what you would pay in the United States, and the persuasive sales agent seems to have all the information. As an added bonus, the agent will provide property management services at a modest 10 percent monthly fee, which includes everything from collecting rents, making repairs, and keeping it occupied. In fact, the property is only worth $125,000. So for the next year, you're receiving the money you expected, which is coming from the $125,000 that your overpaid, and you're remitting 10 percent back to the agent for the privilege. After a year, the tenant, if there ever was one, supposedly moves or decides to pay you less, and the sales agent says there's nothing to be done. After all, the guarantee was only for a year. If you try to sell the property back to the sales agent or a third party, you may find out what the true value of the property is. Again, due diligence would have reduced the possibility of this happening to you.

But He Spoke My Language

Just this year I read an article in the German press that typifies how foreign investors can be taken. What happened to Manfred in Germany is not unique and serves as a reminder of how important it is to take the proper steps to make your offshore real estate investment a reality rather than a nightmare.

Manfred, who is now sixty-seven, had dreams of retiring to Malaga, Spain. He began building his retirement home in the sun in 1999 when he handed over €250,000 to a contractor to finish what was then a bare frame. Manfred had it all planned out: The new home would serve as a rental property, providing him income until he was ready to retire at age sixty-five. Eight years after his initial investment, the "home" is still in its original construction state, and Manfred is in an ongoing legal process to get his home built or at least get his money back. Manfred located the contractor, who had declared bankruptcy but continued in the construction business under different names and entities, using loopholes in Spanish law to avoid being held accountable by all the clients he had left in the lurch. If it's any consolation, Manfred is not alone. Legions of investors have found themselves involved in matters of shoddy construction or nonexistent properties.

Spain is the number one destination for German retirees and, as a result, has become a haven for those who want to take advantage of novice investors. Corruption in the construction industry is a daily event in Spain. In Marbella, at least 30,000 homes were built illegally. The city council is in the midst of a huge corruption scandal regarding this matter, two dozen persons are in jail, and the town is in financial ruin. In a vacation spot close to Marbella, the mayor is in jail for corruption. In Barcelona, over a thousand people were defrauded, putting up money for nonexistent homes. Some investors are finding that properties they bought are being sold again before they can record the deed at the registry. Others are buying properties on streets that do not exist or purchasing homes that have no access to water or have substandard electrical systems.

Consequently, many investors are beginning to look elsewhere for vacation and retirement homes. Not only have they heard about the corruption, but Spain's overbuilding is turning acres of undeveloped land into concrete jungles. Due to the high number of people being taken advantage of, the Spanish government has begun to recognize that these issues exist and to develop regulations for commercial builders.

Looking back, Manfred wishes he would have spoken at least a little Spanish so that he could have initially retained a Spanish attorney regarding his investment and retirement plans. At the time, he had fully trusted the builder, who was a German contractor. "I thought because he was German and spoke my language that I could trust him," said Manfred. In the end, you need to be in charge of your investment, regardless of how convincing the seller is—even if you are old friends or acquaintances, or speak the same language.

After Manfred's disaster, the German Protection League for Foreign Properties passed on these pointers to assist others:

- There is a difference between Spanish law and German law. (Of course, you can replace "Spanish" and "German" with any two countries.)
- In Spain, un-notarized contracts are valid.
- The most recent contract is the one that is valid.
- Read all documents completely before signing. (If you don't know the language, work with someone who does.)
- For new construction, do not pay all the money upfront. Only make payments when you have verified that the phase of the construction is completed. Make sure that any third party who is making payments for you is trustworthy.

- Ensure that the seller has paid all real and personal property taxes, or that you are aware of what they are and your obligation to pay them.
- Run to the register of deeds!
- The first price is not the last price. Negotiate.
- Not all vacation rentals are cash flowing. Do the numbers; don't let your desires overtake reality.
- Understand the consequences of inheritance and what the inheritance taxes are.

These and many other items should be in the forefront of your mind when acquiring offshore properties.

Regions and Countries of Interest to Investors

As mentioned, there are many factors involved when determining where to invest. The following countries represent some of the places that have been of interest to global investors. They represent a variety of possibilities and investment entry levels, some posing a higher risk than others. The taxation issues of these countries vary widely. In all cases, the amount of time the property is held, for what purpose, and by which kind of entity are important factors in determining tax freedom. As always, before making a decision, you should do your due diligence and thoroughly investigate your choice.

Based on a recent study conducted by Jones Lang LaSalle, $237 billion was directly invested in global real estate in the first half of 2005, representing an 18% increase from a year before. North America accounted for 53% of all transactions. Asia Pacific real estate investment continued to experience the strongest growth in total transactions.

Central America

Costa Rica

Government
One of the oldest democracies in South America, as well as being a free and independent republic, Costa Rica maintains political stability with a long-standing commitment to democratic freedom. Peace is Costa Rica's most valued feature: The country has no army; the civil and rural guard ensure that citizens are protected.

Society
Costa Rica has a compulsory state-paid educational system; private institutions at all levels are also available. The literacy rate is 93%. The government also funds medical programs. Spanish is the primary language. English, French, German, and Italian are also spoken. Catholicism is the official religion.

Geography
Costa Rica is a small tropical country situated between the Pacific Ocean and Caribbean Sea. It contains a diverse topography of rivers, plains, mountains, valleys, volcanoes, and beaches. Habitats range from tropical dry forest to lowland rainforest. Costa Rica is recognized for its natural resource conservation activities.

Economy

Costa Rica has a stable economy, primarily dependent on tourism, agriculture, and electronics exports. It has the second largest gross domestic product (GDP) per capita in South America. Poverty has decreased over the past fifty years.

The government implemented a seven-year plan of expansion in the high-tech industry, offering tax exemptions to corporations willing to invest in the country. Several global high-tech corporations are currently participating, including chip manufacturer Intel, pharmaceutical company Glaxo Smith Kline, and consumer products company Procter & Gamble.

Costa Rica is negotiating free trade agreements with Canada and the Dominican Republic. A number of bilateral investment treaties have been signed with other countries.

Types of Investments

Most foreign investment is in the industrial sector, primarily reinvestments in existing companies rather than the arrival of new companies. Real estate developments, including hotels, golf courses, and marinas, have been rising dramatically in value.

Shoreline properties are owned by the government. You need a concession to develop, which is granted for five to twenty years. Foreigners have restrictions on concessions, such as they must live in the country for five years as a legal resident. Corporations cannot have more than 50% ownership. There are certain ecological restrictions on land near natural forests. There are also building restrictions on new construction and renovations.

Mineral rights are owned by the government.

Who Is Involved in Real Estate Transactions

Real estate agents are involved in the initial transaction. A lawyer or notary (notaries are lawyers) prepares the sale agreement in the form of a public deed and verifies the information in accordance with the Notary Code. Corporations must provide a certificate of incorporation. An affidavit of the public deed (known as a *testi-monio*) is filed with the National Property Registry, with proof of payment of the transfer tax and other applicable stamp taxes. If the transfer deed complies with all the requirements, it is recorded, and the buyer becomes the property owner. If the document contains problems, it is returned to the notary for correction and refiling.

Payment Methods

Funds can be transferred online or by wire. Transfer tax and stamp duties must be paid either online or in person to the Banco de Costa Rica, a state-owned bank that transfers the money to the tax authorities. To pay online, you must have a bank account and Internet access to the bank's secure website. The notary certifies on the affidavit that the payment was made, and the registrant must check that on the bank's database.

Title

Title can be held individually, jointly, in trust, as a household, or by a corporation. For estate planning purposes, a corporation is recommended. Properties are registered with the National Registry. The seller obtains a certification from the National Registry, which lists such things as the type of property, location, owner, liens, and mortgages. If the certification is in the computer database, it can be obtained online in one day. However, some properties may be still recorded on the old property books. In that case, it takes eight days to get a written certification.

Title insurance is available, but it does not fully secure a property investment.

Taxes and Fees

Real estate agent or broker: 5% to 10% of purchase price
Stamp taxes, registry and notary fees, and transfer tax: 1.5%
Annual property tax: approximately 0.6%

Required Personal Documents
Copy of your passport; residency card where applicable

Buying a Single-Family Dwelling
The following lists the minimum time needed under optimum conditions and the approximate costs to complete the purchase of a dwelling after the offer has been accepted.

	Days	Cost in U.S. $
Obtain certification online from the National Registry	1 (8 days if not online)	1
Obtain cadastre	1	2
Obtain tax clearance certificate from the municipality	2	2
Notary drafts the sale agreement as a public deed	2	2,700
Pay transfer tax and stamp duties to Banco de Costa Rica	1	5,300
File public deed with the National Registry	15	0
Total	22 days	$8,005

Insurance
Insurance can be obtained through the National Insurance Institute.

Debt Financing
Regular mortgages; bond mortgages; U.S. banks; bond market with a multitude of private investors

Inheritance
If there are no heirs, the property reverts to the government.

Foreign Investment Issues

Urban leaseholds apply to office space, single-family residences, and commercial and industrial uses. For industrial uses, the tenant is protected by statute and is impossible to evict. Farms and agricultural property are arranged by contractual agreement, but unregistered leases are also common. A legal complaint filed over a contract takes an average of 550 days to resolve.

For more information

www.camaracbr.or.cr
The website for the Costa Rican Real Estate Association provides contacts for real estate brokers and real estate professionals as well as links to listings.

www.amcham.co.cr
The Costa Rican–American Chamber of Commerce advocates increased trade and investment between the United States and Costa Rica.

El Salvador

Government

El Salvador has a stable democratic government, modest economic growth, and declining poverty rates. Crimes against persons and property continue to be problems.

Society

Spanish is the primary language, although English is spoken by a small number of people in the capital. English is primarily spoken by professionals or those in the tourist industry, as well as by deported gangsters of Salvadoran origin removed from major U.S. cities such as Los Angeles. Ninety-six percent of the population is Catholic. Education is free through ninth grade. The national literacy rate is 84%.

Geography

El Salvador is the smallest and most densely populated country on the continent. It is the only Central American country that does not have a Caribbean coastline. Only the Lempa River, flowing from Honduras across El Salvador to the ocean, is navigable for commercial traffic. In 1998, Hurricane Mitch devastated the country, damaging about 20% of the housing and leaving over 30,000 homeless. El Salvador also has frequent earthquakes.

Economy

The government has made a commitment to free market initiatives and conservative fiscal management that includes the privatization of the banking system, telecommunications, public pensions, electrical distribution, and some electrical generation. It has also reduced import duties, eliminated price controls, and improved the enforcement of intellectual property rights. It is the most industrialized nation in the region.

El Salvador uses the U.S. dollar as its currency.

Types of Investment

There are restrictions on landownership for foreigners. A foreigner may purchase up to 245 hectares only if there is a reciprocal agreement with the buyer's home country. Foreign direct investments in commerce, certain services, and fishing have limits. Investments in railroads, piers, and canals need government approval. Resident corporations get a favorable fixed income tax rate, and benefits also exist for investors in free trade zone areas (primarily industrial).

Most investors are from the United States and Central and South America.

Who Is Involved in Real Estate Transactions

There are no licensing laws. Bolsa Inmobiliaria is a private property listing system. The real estate profession is well known and accepted. Exclusive listings are only about 20% of the market. Data on new residential properties is published regularly in magazines. A notary prepares and notarizes the sale agreement (notaries must be lawyers). The parties are responsible for gathering all the documentation to be presented to the notary.

The public deed is filed at the respective municipality for calculation of municipal taxes. The title is valid even if it is not filed at the municipality. The incentive to file lies on the previous owner, who continues to pay the taxes on the property if it is not filed. The filing can take from one to five days.

Payment Methods

The registration fee and transfer tax must be paid at a commercial bank.

Title

Title can be held as an individual or other entity, such as a corporation or limited liability company. The public deed is filed at the Register of Property under the name of the buyer. The deed is registered in ten to twenty working days. If you make a premium payment with the registry, certain services and documents can be obtained within two to eight working days. The premium payment is a fixed amount deposited in a special account. The buyer sets up the account.

Taxes and Fees

Notarization and sales agreement: 0.15% to 1% of purchase price
Registration and transfer fees: 0.63% of price, plus 3% of amount
    over $28,571.43
Real property tax: 13%

Required Personal Documents

A photocopy of personal identification and the tax identification numbers of the parties are required. If the purchaser is a corporation, a photocopy of the corporate documents (articles of incorporation, credentials) and tax identification number are necessary. A copy of the property title or Literal Certification (LC) and proof of payment of municipal taxes are also required.

Buying a Single-Family Dwelling

The following lists the minimum time needed under optimum conditions and the approximate costs to complete the purchase of a dwelling after the offer has been accepted.

	Days	Cost in U.S. $
Obtain a Literal Certification and a Non-Lien Certification of the property at the Register of Property	3	10
Obtain tax clearance (*solvencia de renta*) from the Treasury (Ministerio de Hacienda)	2	0
Prepare and notarize the sale agreement	3	700
Pay registration fees and transfer tax at a commercial bank	1	3,500
Register deed at Registry office	21	0
File public deed at the respective municipality	3	70
Total	33 days	$4,280

Foreign Investment Issues

The government can expropriate private property for public utility reasons. According to the Land Policy Network of the World Bank, property rights are not fully secure. New laws should improve land registration procedures and provide more security in land titling. You have the right of recourse to the local judiciary to resolve disputes, which is slow, expensive, and often results in doubtful outcomes. The court system works mostly with written rather than oral arguments. Graft and monetary corruption may play a role in decision making.

Although El Salvador has also made progress in reducing the bureaucracy that has negatively affected foreign trade and investment, foreign investors still face cumbersome administrative procedures, such as the requirement to register with the Ministry of Economy. Investment permission and registration procedures can take months, and information regarding these procedures can be hard to obtain as well as contradictory.

Foreign investors may hold dollar accounts in El Salvador and use these accounts when seeking local financing. Fifty percent of net profits in commercial and service industries can be remitted legally—100% in practice. When a business is terminated, there are no restrictions on the repatriation of funds as long as they are in proportion to what was initially invested.

For more information

www.elnoble.com/legal.htm
This Spanish-language website offers legal and financial information as well as comparative information for different properties. The organization is associated with other real estate organizations and has an office in Los Angeles.

www.cnr.gob.sv/ct_introduccion.htm
This is the website for the National Registry (Centro Nacional de Registros) and Catastro.

www.tufuturacasa.com/guide/financiamiento.html
This Spanish-language guide on the process involved in purchasing real estate provides contact information and also lists properties.

Guatemala

Government
Guatemala has a serious problem with the inequality of land distribution, an issue that was a significant motivating factor in its civil war. Land has been the source of political conflict for generations, since the colonial and then republican governments divided up the

land of Guatemala's indigenous people to reward and maintain the
loyalty of their supporters. Two percent of the population own large
tracts of land, while 98% own no arable farmland at all. Because of
this disparity, Guatemalan rural workers' organizations have seized
unused estates with the intent of making the government purchase
the land and distribute it as small farm-holdings.

According to a 2004 report by the U.S. Department of Commerce:
"Though Guatemala passed a foreign investment law in 1998 to
streamline and facilitate foreign investment, time-consuming administrative procedures, arbitrary bureaucratic impediments and judicial
decisions, a high crime rate and corruption impede investment."

Society

Although the official language is Spanish, it is not universally spoken
among the indigenous population nor is it often spoken as a second
language. Twenty-one distinct Mayan languages are still spoken,
especially in rural areas. The government runs a number of public
elementary and secondary schools. These schools are theoretically
tuition free, but the cost of uniforms, books, supplies, and transportation makes them less accessible to the lower classes.

More than 54% of Guatemala's population is considered poor,
and 23% to 27% are considered extremely poor, a situation that has
been exacerbated by the drought and loss of jobs resulting from a
decline in coffee exports.

Geography

Guatemala is mountainous, except for the south coastal area and the
northern vast lowlands. Its climate is hot tropical, more temperate in
the highlands, and drier in the easternmost regions. All major cities
are in the southern half of the country. Its location on the Caribbean
Sea and Pacific Ocean makes it a target for hurricanes.

Economy

The agricultural sector accounts for one-quarter of the GDP, two-thirds
of exports, and half of the labor force. Coffee, sugar, and bananas are

the main exports. Manufacturing and construction account for 20% of GDP. Challenges include increasing government revenues, negotiating further assistance from international donors, and increasing the efficiency and openness of both government and private financial operations. In 2005, Guatemala's congress ratified the Dominican Republic–Central American Free Trade Agreement (DR-CAFTA) between several Central American nations and the United States.

Types of Investments

Mainly Americans invest in vacation homes, villas, and small businesses. Prices average $65,000 to $300,000. Foreigners can acquire, maintain, and dispose of real property with very few restrictions. Foreign investors are also allowed to repatriate profits and capital without restriction.

Foreigners cannot own land directly next to rivers, oceans, or international borders. Minerals, petroleum, and natural resources are considered the property of the state.

Foreign firms developing projects in designated tourism zones are eligible for income tax exemption on revenue from their investments and duty-free importation of any needed goods or materials not made in Central America.

Who Is Involved in Real Estate Transactions

Realtor licensing is not required; however, commissions licensing does exist. A lawyer/notary prepares the sale agreement and notarizes it by preparing the public deed. The seller is responsible for gathering all the documentation to be presented to the lawyer. The notary is in charge of buying the state stamps for the value-added tax (VAT) payment if necessary and adhering the stamps to the public deed.

Payment Methods

Residents and nonresidents may hold foreign exchange accounts, and you can transfer funds into the country.

Title

The seller obtains a certificate at the Property Registry. It is important to verify that the property has no encumbrances and is owned by the seller. The actualized certificate is used to prepare the public deed. The registry number where the property is registered, which can be obtained from the seller or an electronic certificate, is required.

Taxes and Fees

Value-added tax: 12% of the purchase price, if necessary
Annual property tax: 0 to 9%
Business tax: 5% of taxable income
Long-term capital gains tax: 10%
Short-term capital gains: 31%

Required Personal Documents

Photocopies of the IDs of the seller and buyer (copy of passport or local ID) are required. If you are using a corporation or other entity, a corporate resolution or similar action indicating the resolution to purchase property is required to transfer property.

Buying a Single-Family Dwelling

The following lists the minimum time needed under optimum conditions to complete the purchase of a dwelling after the offer has been accepted.

	Days
Verify property registry (depends on size of the real estate file or if it is digitalized)	11
Obtain cadastre value	1
Prepare public deed	2
Deliver public deed to registry	14
Notify the municipality of the transaction	10
Total	38 days

Debt Financing
Mortgage financing is either not available or can be extremely expensive (up to 20%).

Foreign Investment Issues
Beware of squatters taking possession of your property.

For more information
www.ccbrg.net
The Guatemalan Brokers Real Estate Chamber (CCBRG) sponsors activities for the improvement and development of those involved in real estate.

Honduras

Government
Democratic governance and a market economy continue to survive in Honduras, despite pervasive poverty, violent crime, and a weak judicial system. According to the U.S. Department of Commerce, the investment climate is hampered by high levels of corruption, a troubled financial sector, and limited infrastructure. The constitution requires that all foreign investment complement, but not substitute for, national investment.

Society
Most of the population lives in the western part of the interior highlands and the Caribbean lowlands. Northeastern Honduras is sparsely settled. About 50% of the population is rural but is rapidly urbanizing. Unemployment is about 28%; 45% of the population lives in extreme poverty. There is a high degree of malnutrition, and infant and child mortality rates are also high. Medical care is minimal for most of the population. Honduras is predominantly Roman Catholic, although Protestant denominations are increasing rapidly.

Geography

The region is considered a biodiversity hotspot with numerous plant and animal species. Like the other countries in the region, Honduras contains vast biological resources, including lush rain forests, untouched cloud forests, mangroves, savannas, and mountain ranges. The country was devastated by Hurricane Mitch in 1998.

Economy

The economy is based mostly on agriculture. The maquiladora sector is the third-largest in the world. The country's international reserve position continues to be strong. The local currency, the lempira, was devalued for many years but stabilized against the U.S. dollar in 2005.

Types of Investments

There are over 10,000 U.S. citizens living in Honduras full time, mostly in the capital city of Tegucigalpa. Foreigners, mostly from the United States and Canada, are increasingly investing in second homes, especially in the Bay Islands of Roatan, Utila, and Guanaja. The number of foreigners purchasing real estate in tourism areas is expected to multiply in the coming years.

An individual can own up to three-quarters of an acre. By forming a corporation with a Honduran lawyer, you can increase that amount. There are two kinds of corporations that allow you to buy land: limited partnerships and stock corporations. The corporation retains full ownership of the property, and you are entitled to the same rights as a Honduran citizen regarding property ownership. As a corporation, you face no restrictions on building or developing your land.

Many U.S. firms have large manufacturing operations, mainly in San Pedro Sula, where large industrial parks with special benefits (duty-free, tax free, capital repatriation, and so on) are located. When purchasing property for development, you need to have feasibility and environmental impact studies, which may take many months to complete.

Foreigners purchasing in tourism zones exceeding 3,000 square meters need to apply with the Ministry of Tourism. Foreign ownership of land near the coast or along borders is generally prohibited but may be allowed in some cases with government permission. Government authorization is required for foreign investment in basic health services, telecommunications, electricity, air transport, fishing and hunting, exploration and exploitation of minerals, forestry, agriculture, insurance and financial services, and private education.

Who Is Involved in Real Estate Transactions

A notary, who is an attorney, is responsible for authorizing every transaction you make, including the title search. You cannot buy title insurance in Honduras, so be sure to hire a reputable lawyer to do your title search.

Taxes and Fees

Transfer tax: 1.5% of sales price

Property taxes: Average 0.25%. If you are involved with a government-approved tourism project, you pay no income tax on your profits for twenty years.

Income tax declarations: Must be filed by individuals and corporations. A simple filing costs about $350.

Required Personal Documents

A copy of your passport, local identification, or birth certificate is required.

Debt Financing

Most domestic banks are family run and are tightfisted in their lending practices. Often, only affiliated businesses and individuals are granted credit. State-owned bank operations have been sharply reduced in recent years.

For more information

www.amcham.hn2.com/aboutus.htm

The Honduran American Chamber of Commerce is an independent, voluntary, nonprofit organization of business executives concerned with local community services and United States trade and investment.

Nicaragua

Government

Nicaragua is a young democracy with a developing economy. The judicial system is subject to corruption and political influence. Protection of property rights is weak, and property disputes are among the most serious barriers to investment.

Society

Approximately 76% of the population is mestizo, 10% European, 3% indigenous, and 11% Creole or African. Spanish is the official language, spoken by almost everyone in the Pacific lowlands and central highlands. English is the predominant language in the Caribbean lowlands. Miskito is the predominant indigenous language.

Education is free and the literacy is about 77%. The health-care system is inadequate, despite modest improvement during the 1980s. Approximately 70% of the population is below the poverty line, with nearly 50% unemployed or underemployed. Access to safe drinking water and basic public services is generally poor, especially in rural areas and the Caribbean coast. The quality of housing is poor in urban shantytowns, and there is an acute housing shortage in the capital.

Geography

The climate is generally hot and humid, with the "summer" dry season running mid-November through mid-May and the "winter" rainy season running from mid-May through mid-November. Terrain ranges from the hilly and volcanic to coastal beaches and tropical jungles.

Economy

Nicaragua is attempting to attract investment, create jobs, and reduce poverty by opening the economy to foreign trade. It is primarily an agricultural country, but construction, mining, fisheries, and general commerce have expanded during the last few years. In recent years, tourism has rapidly grown, becoming Nicaragua's third-largest industry to attract capital from outside sources.

Types of Investments

The vacation home market is beginning to boom. The Pacific coast and the shores of Lake Nicaragua are seen as the areas with strong vacation market development possibilities. Foreign investors mainly from the United States and Canada are also beginning to invest in second homes. This is anticipated to increase in the coming years because of the current low cost of coastal real estate compared with other nearby second-home hot spots such as Costa Rica.

There are no restrictions on foreign ownership. Citizens and nonresidents have the same rights of ownership.

Average Price of Real Property

It is difficult to judge market values, as information for price comparisons is not formally available. Some examples are $80,000 for two acres of beachfront property; $280,000 for a three-bedroom beachfront home; $50,000 to $450,000 for residential property.

Who Is Involved in Real Estate Transactions

Most transactions are done directly between the buyer and seller, and agents are not involved. If you are familiar with Nicaraguan real estate and speak fluent Spanish, you could buy directly from the local farmer or property owner. However, it is strongly recommended that you enlist the help of a reputable local attorney to check the title before making any deposit. Property titles all over the country are in dispute, and people have tried to sell land they did not actually own. Sometimes it is a good idea to have two attorneys check the title: a local attorney and one from a firm in Managua. Title registers are maintained locally.

Real estate transactions are usually overseen by a notary. The position of notary is the highest level of attorney qualification and is awarded by the government. The buyer usually selects the notary, who is paid by the seller. After you have agreed upon a purchase price with the seller, the notary prepares a *promesa de venta* (promise to sell). This is a three-party agreement, signed by the buyer, seller, and notary. It is essential that you obtain an enforceable contract with an agreed-on purchase price. After the agreement is executed, the notary prepares a *testimonio*. This is an exact copy of the *promesa* and is placed in the public records to advise other prospective real estate buyers that the property is under contract.

When all conditions of the *promesa* have been met, the notary prepares an *escritura* (deed) to be executed by the buyer, seller, and notary. Another *testimonio* is prepared. An appraisal of the property is done after it is registered. After the transfer taxes have been paid, the *testimonio* is recorded in the Public Registry office at the local municipality.

Payment Method
Payments are made via wire transfer.

Title
Title can be held individually, jointly, in trust, as household property, or by corporations. Property ownership is fee simple or freehold.

Taxes and Fees
Notary: 1.5% to 2% of property price

Property registration: 0.5% of cadastral value

Transfer tax: 4% of purchase price. Most sellers ask the buyer to pay it. Because the transfer tax is actually a prepayment of income tax, the buyer is the only one to benefit from paying it.

Annual property taxes: 1% of the assessed value. Farmland up to 42.6 hectares is exempt. Some territories are tax exempt. Luxury tax is applicable in some cases. In general, taxes are relatively low.

If you are starting a business, you can open a tourism-related business and pay no taxes for ten years, as well as purchase all the supplies you need tax free.

Foreign retirees pay no taxes on out-of-country earnings. Any income originating from within Nicaragua is taxed at a flat 15%. Income from local sources are taxed progressively to a maximum of 35%. Capital gains and earnings from rental property are treated as taxable income. Retirees are entitled to:

- Bring up to $10,000 worth of household goods duty-free for their own use.
- Import one car for personal or general use and pay no import tax or protective tariff. If the car is sold after five years, it is exempt from consumer sales tax.
- Import an additional vehicle every five years under the same tax exemption.

Required Personal Documents

You need a copy of your birth certificate and passport. If you are planning to live in Nicaragua, you need a certificate or letter from your doctor stating that you are in good physical health, free from communicable diseases, and mentally sound; a letter from your local police department stating that you have never been convicted of any crime; a certificate of income from your bank or pension plan affirming that you will have enough money to meet the minimum requirement of $400 a month; and a list of the household items that you will be importing. These documents must all be translated into Spanish by a lawyer and notarized.

Buying a Single-Family Dwelling

The following lists the minimum time needed under optimum conditions and the approximate costs to complete the purchase of a dwelling after the offer has been accepted.

	Days	Cost in U.S. $
Obtain nonencumbrance certificate	5	10
Obtain tax clearance certificate from the municipality	1	2
Notary prepares and signs the public deed	2	800
Obtain cadastre certificate and valuation at the Cadastre	10	20
Inspector visits property to assess value	7	0
Pay income/transfer tax	1	455
Insert documents obtained from the Cadastre in public deed	1	70
Apply for registration of the public deed at the Land Registry	46	260
Total	73 days	$1,617

Insurance

Real property insurance covering fire and earthquake is available.

Debt Financing

Like most Central American countries, local financing is almost unheard of, and when it is available, it is on less than appealing terms. In 2005, loan rates averaged 13.2%. Depending on your situation, you might choose to take advantage of developer financing or arrange a loan through your U.S. bank. The secondary mortgage market is developing.

For more information
www.canibir.com/es/index.php
This Spanish-language website for the Nicaraguan chamber of real
estate brokers (CNCBR) lists members and events.

Panama

Government

Once a part of Colombia, Panama has been independent since 1903.
Its canal was built by the United States in the early twentieth century
and operated jointly with the United States until 1999. Much of
Panama's domestic politics and international relations in the twentieth century were tied to the Panama Canal and the foreign policy of
the United States. Relations between the United States and Panama
became very strained in 1987 because of allegations of President
Manuel Noreiga's (an ex-member of the CIA) involvement in drug
trafficking and money laundering. In 1989, the U.S. military invaded
Panama and ousted Noreiga. Today, Panama manages the canal and
has put former U.S. military zones to commercial use. President
Martín Torrijos, elected in 2004, has enacted laws to curb corruption
and has proposed expanding the canal to handle large container ships.
Panama is also giving more attention to other commercial and trade
relations and especially to the Central American peace process.

Society

There are three principal ethnic groups: Spanish-speaking mestizos,
representing the vast majority of inhabitants; English-speaking An-
tillean blacks, constituting approximately 8% of the population; and
tribal Indians, making up about 5% of the population. Spanish is the
official language. The dominant religion is Roman Catholicism.

Education is free at public primary, secondary, and high schools
and compulsory. Over 90% of the population is literate. Most med-

ical facilities and personnel are located in major urban areas, but most people have ready access to medical care of some kind. The life expectancy is about seventy-two years.

Geography

Central and South America are connected by Panama's narrow land bridge, or isthmus, which at its narrowest is fifty kilometers wide. Its north coast lies along the Caribbean, and its southern coastline is on the Pacific Ocean. The climate is tropical with basically two seasons: a hot and humid rainy season (May to January) and a dry season (January to May). It rains approximately seventy-six inches per year in Panama City, the nation's capital. Near the Panamanian coast there are 1,600 islands. Tropical rain forests run along the Panama Canal, the Darien Gap, and the eastern half of the country. The west coast is predominately grassland, and the highlands have alpine vegetation and mountain forests.

Economy

Panama is a financial hub in Latin America and home to numerous international companies and financial institutions. The banking sector is very successful, in large part because the U.S. dollar is the national currency. This has allowed Panama to maintain one of the lowest inflation rates in Latin America, one that often has been lower than that of the United States. Panama hosts branches from almost every major bank around the world and is ranked as the second-best place in Latin America to access capital. A 1998 banking reform law brought Panamanian regulations largely into compliance with international standards. There are few restrictions on opening banks, and the government exercises little control over the allocation of credit. Domestic and foreign banks, which are treated equally, offer a wide variety of financial services.

The government controls pharmaceutical and fuel prices. It also influences prices through state-owned enterprises and utilities, including electricity and water. Panama also offers a retirement program to encourage retirees to settle in Panama. The *pensionado* program provides numerous benefits, including discounts ranging from medical expenses and home loans to entertainment and transportation costs.

Types of Investments

Because of the government's efforts and incentives, many people invest in retirement homes. The government imposes some limitations on foreign ownership, for example, in the retail and media sectors ownership must be Panamanian, except in cases of franchising. Foreign investors also may not purchase land within ten kilometers of a national border or on an island. Otherwise, foreign and national investors have equal rights in terms of investments and business practices.

Foreign investment is welcomed and may be freely repatriated. With a minimum investment of $50,000 anywhere in Panama's interior, you can receive a twenty-year exemption on import taxes for materials, furniture, equipment, and vehicles; a twenty-year exemption on real estate taxes for all assets of the enterprise; an exemption from any tax levied for the use of airports and piers; and an accelerated depreciation for real estate assets of 10% per year. If you start up a tourism-related business in one of the specially designated tourist zones, you can also receive a fifteen-year exemption on income taxes.

Who Is Involved in Real Estate Transactions

Real estate brokers must have a professional license issued by the real estate board. A Promissory Letter of Purchase (*Carta de Promesa de Compra Venta*) outlines the terms of the transaction between the buyer and the seller, as well as between the seller and the real estate agent. All transactions should be registered with the Public Registry. A notary executes this registration and is responsible for verifying all the necessary steps and data. Contracts are governed by the Civil Code and are only enforceable by law if they are of public record and authorized by a certified notary. Both the grantor and the grantee must sign the transfer deed at the same time, with two witnesses and before a notary. Attorneys can represent the parties involved. It takes approximately forty days to complete a transaction.

Payment Methods

There is no escrow and no title insurance, although a secure transaction can be made through a local bank. Both residents and nonresidents may hold foreign exchange accounts. There are no restrictions or controls on payments, transactions, transfers, repatriation of profits, or capital transactions.

Title

Title may be held as individuals, corporations, partnerships, joint ventures, and trusts. A deed is used to transfer title, which must be notarized. The notary keeps the original copy, and the parties involved receive certified copies. The deed is recorded in the Public Record. Panama does not keep a computerized record of property ownership.

Taxes and Fees

Commission for real estate agent: 5% of purchase price is customary, but is negotiable; paid by the seller

Transfer tax: 2%

Gains in sale of real estate are considered income, but they are computed on a separate basis.

Because Panama does not have an automated system for property transactions and income, it is difficult to track property transfers and easy to conceal information from the government. As a result, putting properties under fraudulent names to conceal ownership is illegally practiced to avoid taxation.

Required Personal Documents

The following documents are required: a job letter and copy of two pay slips (for borrowers currently earning a salary); a copy of the last three personal income tax declarations and/or business income tax declarations or audited financial statements; two copies of ID cards or passports (all pages in the passport must be copied); adequate verification of sufficient personal assets (copy of bank account statements, real estate titles, bonds, common stock, etc.); a copy of the purchase agreement; credit references.

Insurance

Property holders can purchase fire insurance, crop insurance, mortgage insurance, life insurance, accident insurance, and insurable insurance.

Debt Financing

Mortgages are available for 60% to 70% of the purchase price or appraised market value, whichever is less; the specific rates and conditions may vary from bank to bank.

Inheritance

An estate passes in the following order in the event of death: (1) descendants in equal parts; (2) ascendants in equal parts. There is no estate tax or duty. The municipality of the deceased's last place of residence takes the entire estate if there are no heirs.

Foreign Investment Issues

The government may take a property with compensation for a public utility or social interest as defined by law. Panama has rent control and monitors rises in rent. The lessee is not responsible for repairs and if repairs take more than forty days, the lessee is not required to pay rent.

For more information

www.acobir.com
This is the Spanish-language website of the Panamanian Association of Real Estate Brokers and Developers (ACOBIR).

www.businesspanama.com
This website provides links to articles and information that promote investing in Panama.

Caribbean

Barbados

Government
Barbados is an independent nation in the British Commonwealth with a parliamentary democracy modeled on the British system. Executive authority is vested in the prime minister and cabinet, which is collectively responsible to the parliament. The prime minister is the head of the winning party, as selected through majority vote. The prime minister usually chooses a cabinet from his party members in the legislature. The present government is proposing that Barbados become a republic, with a ceremonial president replacing the British sovereign. This issue is being hotly debated because the island has been autonomous for decades, and the Crown's position is strictly nominal.

Society
More than 90% of the population is of African descent, consisting mostly of descendants of the slave laborers on the sugar plantations. English is the official language, and a nonstandard English called Bajan is spoken. Most Barbadians are Protestant, chiefly of the Anglican Church. Since the 1950s, the rate of population growth has been slowed by a successful family-planning program and by emigration, mostly to other parts of the Caribbean and to North America. In the same period, the death and infant mortality rates declined

sharply, and life expectancy rose above seventy years. Barbados has one of the highest standards of living and literacy rates in the developing world. Barbados is internationally known for cricket and hosted the 2007 Cricket World Cup.

Geography

Barbados is a relatively flat island, with a tropical climate and constant trade winds off the Atlantic Ocean. It lies just outside the principal hurricane belt. It is a nonvolcanic island composed of limestone coral; erosion has removed the coral cover. The government has adopted a conservation plan to prevent further erosion. The fauna has been highly degraded by humans, with many native species disappearing. Sugarcane estates dot the island.

Economy

Historically, the Barbadian economy had been dependent on sugarcane cultivation and related activities, but production in recent years has diversified into light industry and tourism. Tourism is the most important economic sector. Offshore finance and information services are important foreign exchange earners. Although the offshore financial sector is smaller than others in the Caribbean, it makes a significant contribution to the economy and is generally well regulated. The government continues its efforts to reduce unemployment, to encourage direct foreign investment, and to privatize state-owned enterprises. Since the late 1990s, the island has had a construction boom with the development and redevelopment of hotels, office complexes, and homes. Barbados emphasizes economic and cultural cooperation within the Caribbean region and the development of a common trade policy position within the Caribbean Community and Common Market (CARICOM) trade bloc.

Types of Investments

The government has an aggressive program for attracting foreign investment and grants special concessions and incentives if you are building for the tourism market. This applies to restaurants; recreational facilities and services; development of attractions that emphasize the island's natural, historic, and cultural heritage; and the construction of properties in noncoastal areas.

Buying into a resort development is becoming an increasingly popular option. Some are gated communities with varied communal facilities. Although the most sought after properties are beachfront locations on the island's west coast, many investors are turning to the countryside and buying traditional Barbadian plantation houses and country villas.

Foreign nationals have the same legal protections as domestic investors. However, foreign investors must get government approval for their investments and need to register their investments with the country's Central Bank to ensure the free repatriation of their profits and capital.

Who Is Involved in Real Estate Transactions

No license is needed to purchase property. However, all nonresidents, whether persons or offshore companies, must obtain permission from the Exchange Control Authority to purchase property. Normally, such permission is granted once it is confirmed that foreign currency has been brought into the country and that the transaction is not tainted with illegality.

Purchasing a property involves a sales contract prepared by the seller's attorney. A deposit is made to secure the property, which is held in escrow until completion when the balance of the purchase price is paid and the title passes to the buyer. Between the time of executing the contract and the completion of the sale, the legal representative of the buyer searches the title and ensures that there are no encumbrances, charges, encroachments, or other impediments to the sale. To determine a property's value, the buyer can use a real estate agent without a fee or hire an independent auditor, with fees charged based on the value of the property.

Payment Methods

Funds transferred to Barbados must be registered with the Central Bank of Barbados.

Title

The title may be taken in an individual's name or through a corporate vehicle set up to own the property. It is usual for nonresidents to purchase property through a company that is incorporated outside Barbados but registered to do business in Barbados.

Taxes And Fees

Legal fees: 1% to 4%. Depending on the complexity of the matter involved, fees can be higher. Each party pays their own legal fees.

Transfer tax: none for foreign investors

Commissions and survey costs: paid by seller

Annual land tax: based on the property value

Foreign Investment Issues

Private property is well protected. The legal tradition is based on British common law. By Caribbean standards, the police and court systems are efficient and unbiased, and the government operates in an essentially transparent manner.

Property owners renting for the short-term must apply 7.5% VAT to the rent. Profit derived from rent is subject to income tax.

For more information

www.barbados.gov.bb/Landtax/

This is the official website of the Ministry of Finance-Land Tax Department.

www.barbadosbusiness.gov.bb/miib/Investment/things_to_know.cfm

This is the government website for information on investment opportunities and things you need to know about investing in Barbados.

British Virgin Islands

Government

The British Virgin Islands is a dependent territory of Great Britain and a member of the British Commonwealth. The legal system is based on English common law. The Queen of England is the chief of state, who is represented by an appointed governor. The islands are largely self-governing and rely to a limited extent on British statutes on international matters. Economic ties have been forged with the U.S. Virgin Islands rather than the West Indies Federation of British Territories.

Society

The majority of the population is Afro-Caribbean, descended from the slaves brought to the islands by the British. A small percentage is of British and other European origins. The official language is English. In recent years, immigrants in search of work from other parts of the Caribbean have more than doubled the population. Some relatively minor tensions exist between the newcomers and the "belongers" who see their relaxed lifestyle threatened. Proposals for tough immigration laws are controversial. About 400,000 tourists visit the islands annually, making their presence a dominant feature of the culture. Despite being a British dependent territory, the prevailing cultural influences are more American than British.

Geography

The British Virgin Islands is located a few miles east of the U.S. Virgin Islands. The principal islands are Tortola, Virgin Gorda, Anegada, and Jost Van Dyke. Most of the islands are volcanic in origin and have a hilly, rugged terrain. The climate is subtropical, but the humidity and high temperatures are tempered by cooling trade winds.

Economy

The British Virgin Islands has used the United States dollar as its currency since 1959, although banks maintain accounts in sterling as well. There are no exchange controls. The country has one of the more prosperous economies in the Caribbean region. The two main-stays of the economy are tourism and offshore financial operations. Tourism accounts for an estimated 45% of the national income and employs the most people. The financial services industry contributes 50%, with substantial revenues generated by the registration of offshore companies. More than 600,000 companies are incorporated in the British Virgin Islands, with an average 50,000 new forma-tions taking place every year. The most important offshore activi-ties are trust management, mutual funds, and captive insurance. Banking has not been encouraged as a means to prevent money laundering.

Types of Investments

The majority of land is owned in fee simple. Property can also be held on a long lease from the British Crown or private individuals. The duration of such leases is usually ninety-nine years. Remaining years of preexisting leases can be transferred until the original lease expires, upon which time extensions are renegotiated.

Who Is Involved in Real Estate Transactions

It is essential that the purchaser appoint an attorney for the transac-tion. It is standard practice for the buyer to hold a 10% earnest de-posit in escrow before signing the Sale and Purchase Agreement. The deposit does not bind the seller. An attorney's responsibilities normally include submitting the application for a non-Belonger Landholding License, which is required for nonresident buyers. Four advertisements from a local newspaper stating the property descrip-tion and price must accompany the license application. A buyer should begin processing this application as soon as possible after signing the Sale and Purchase Agreement to adhere to the time limitations. Before property is transferred, the boundaries must be confirmed by the Registrar of Lands. Completion of the transaction usually takes place within thirty days of receipt of the Land Hold License.

Title
A purchaser normally acquires absolute title, which is registered in the Land Registry. Registered titles relate to a detailed Cadastral Survey that defines the legal boundaries.

Taxes and Fees
Annual land tax: $50 for the first half acre or less, $150 on more than half but not exceeding one acre, and $50 on each additional acre

Stamp duty: 12% of the contracted price or appraised value, whichever is higher, for non-Belongers. Belongers pay 4%.

Conveyance fees: 2% of the first $100,000 and 1% of the remaining amount, but not less than $150

House tax: 1.5% of the assessed annual rental value

Rental property: Subject to income taxes. A Trade License is required and the annual fee is $400 for a non-Belonger.

Required Personal Documents
To lease or purchase land, non-Belongers must obtain an Alien Landholding License. Applications for a license require two personal financial references, one bank reference, two character references, police records, an application fee, and a license fee. Licenses carry a two- or three-year commitment to develop unimproved land.

Debt Financing
Some of the banks offer worldwide banking services. Financing up to 75% of the appraised value or the purchase price, whichever is less, is available to foreign investors, subject to status. Construction financing is also available. Mortgages are granted for up to twenty

years. Interest rates are generally 1.5% to 2% above the U.S. prime rate. Banks will also finance the purchase of undeveloped land.

Foreign Investment Issues

Development is governed by planning guidelines that determine general policy. Currently there are no zoning laws, but they are being planned for the near future. Development proposals must be approved by the Land Development Control Authority, which is concerned with government planning, and by the Building Authority, which is responsible for ensuring that buildings are of structurally sound design. It is preferred that the working drawings be prepared and submitted by architects based in the British Virgin Islands.

For more information

www.bvi.gov.vg

Information on investing in property from the Department of Land Registry is available at this website.

Dominican Republic

Government

The Dominican Republic has a multiparty political system with national elections every four years. The military, which consists of about 24,000 active-duty personnel and in the Caribbean is second in size to Cuba's, is commanded by the president. The armed forces are active in efforts to control narcotics as well as illegal immigration from Haiti to the Dominican Republic and from the Dominican Republic to the United States. In recent decades, illegal immigration from Haiti has dramatically increased as the Dominican economy improves and the Haitian economy remains stagnant. Most Haitian immigrants work at low-paying, unskilled labor jobs. The government also plays a major role in the economy, and in the 1990s controversy arose concerning its privatization of many state-owned companies. The government also permitted numerous maquiladoras to be established in tax-free port zones.

Society
The population of the Dominican Republic is predominantly of mixed race, with small black and white minorities. Spanish is the national language, although English is becoming more common because of continued emigration to the United States. Economic problems have led to a vast migration of Dominicans to the United States, mainly to large East Coast cities.

Catholicism is the predominant religion, and the Roman Catholic Church influences all levels of cultural, political, and economic life. About three-fifths of Dominicans remain below the poverty level, despite improvements in the national economy; however, the middle class has grown markedly.

Geography
The Dominican Republic shares the island with Haiti, which occupies the western third of the island. The Caribbean is to the south and the Atlantic Ocean to the north. The Turks and Caicos Islands are 90 miles to the north, and Colombia lies about 300 miles to the south. The Dominican Republic has a moderate, relatively mild tropical climate. The country has many rivers, which it uses for hydroelectric plants.

Economy
In recent years, the service sector has overtaken agriculture (mainly sugarcane, with smaller amounts of coffee, cacao, and tobacco) as the largest employer due to the growth in tourism and free trade zones. Growth turned negative in 2003 with reduced tourism, a major bank fraud, and limited growth in the U.S. economy, which is the source of about 80% of its export revenues, but it recovered in 2004 and 2005. Unemployment remains a challenge. Development prospects have improved with the ratification of the Central America–Dominican Republic Free Trade Agreement (CAFTA-DR) in 2005. Remittances

from the many Dominicans living abroad are also important. The growing economy has accelerated the rate of urbanization and increased the size of the middle class.

Types of Investments

With tourism being the number one industry, a great deal of foreign investment is being made in the development of resort communities. Many foreign nationals have purchased single-family dwellings for vacation purposes or as second homes because of the relatively low cost of living. Some investors are remodeling homes for resale or as rentals to tourists and business people. Many people from different countries are also buying homes for their retirement.

There are no significant restrictions on foreign nationals owning real estate; the country has a long history of foreign nationals being involved in the real estate market. There are controls on how a parcel of real estate may be used, such as zoning, building codes, and subdivision regulations. However, there is no uniform building code.

Who Is Involved in Real Estate Transactions

No license is required to sell real estate in the Dominican Republic. Sellers and buyers can represent themselves or choose anyone to represent them. The buyer bears a fairly heavy due diligence burden when it comes to the purchase of real estate. Property rights are irregularly enforced, and investors often encounter problems in receiving clear title to land. Property ownership information is maintained regionally in the recorder's office, title registrar's office, or land court. This information is publicly available but must be searched by hand. There are currently no computerized records.

The contract for sale must be in writing and signed in front of a notary, who must have a law degree. Contracts are typically drawn by an attorney and must be either in Spanish or translated into Spanish by a judicial translator. The contract for sale sets forth the general terms and conditions of the sale, such as a description of the property, the agreed-on sales price, and the number of days to close the transaction.

The buyer normally posts a deposit of about 10% of the total purchase price. When the contract for sale is signed and notarized, the document is taken to the Internal Revenue Office to determine the taxes owed. Taxes are paid in advance of the final conveyance of the property from the seller to the buyer. The contract for sale and the certificate of title is then filed with the Title Registrar's Office.

Title

In some areas of the country, it can take up to a month before a new title is issued; in other areas, title is issued in one day. Property can be owned as joint tenancy, tenants in common, general partnerships, and limited partnerships. Title insurance is not available.

Taxes and Fees

Transfer fee: about 3% of purchase price, paid by the seller

Property taxes: none

Commissions: mandated by law at 5%, but they are negotiable depending on where you do business; paid by the seller

Attorney fees, document preparation, recording charges, and closing fees: paid by the buyer

Insurance

To protect against loss due to fire and other catastrophic events, lenders require property owners to maintain adequate levels of hazard insurance. Property owners typically desire additional insurance coverage for personal liability and other risks, such as earthquakes, floods, and civil unrest.

Debt Financing

Long-term loans for residential, commercial, and agricultural purposes are available. Short-term loans for personal reasons are available as well but at high interest rates. Loans are guaranteed by title to the property as well as a life insurance policy taken out on the property owner. Lenders look for a minimum loan-to-value ratio and a minimum debt coverage ratio for income-producing properties; however, loans seldom exceed 60% of the value of the real property. Lenders finance loans directly using their own underwriting criteria.

Foreign Investment Issues

Real estate investments have been subject to both legal and physical takeover attempts. Absentee owners of undeveloped land are particularly vulnerable. Investors should seek solid property title and not just a *carta de constancia*, which is often confused by foreigners with a title. An official land registry measurement (also known as a *deslinde* or *mensura catastral*) is also desirable for the cautious overseas investor. The court system is inefficient, and bureaucratic red tape is common. The government can expropriate property arbitrarily. Despite recent judicial reforms, Dominican and foreign business leaders have complained that judicial and administrative corruption affects the settlement of business disputes.

For more information

www.aei.org.do

The Spanish-language website of the Real Estate Association of the Dominican Republic (AEI) represents over eighty estate agencies and other real estate–related companies.

North America

Canada

Government

Canada is formally a constitutional monarchy, with the governor general (always of Canadian nationality and appointed in Ottawa) acting as the representative of the British Crown. In practice, the Canadian House of Commons is sovereign. Canada is a federation of ten provinces, each with substantial powers, and three territories. Canada is a bilingual country, and both French and English are the official languages. One of the main political issues is the lack of a nationwide unity and the provinces' desires for greater autonomy. The separatist Parti Québécois (PQ) first came to power in 1976. Despite losing separatist referendums held in 1980 and 1995, Quebec's sovereignty movement has continued. However, the popularity of the PQ has suffered as voters want to focus on everyday issues rather than the promise of more constitutional wrangling. Any future vote on secession requires federal approval and the agreement of at least seven of the ten provinces. The provinces are responsible for most social programs, such as health care and education. The federal government can initiate policies in provincial areas, which the provinces can opt out of but rarely do. Equalization payments are made by the federal government to ensure that uniform standards of services and taxation are kept between the richer and poorer provinces. Canada offers universal health care.

Society

Canada is ethnically diverse. The largest groups are of English and French descent, but there is also large representation of other Europeans, Chinese, South Asians, and indigenous groups. A variety of religions are practiced; Catholics make up the largest group. The country has one of the highest per capita immigration rates in the world, driven by economic, family reunification, and humanitarian reasons. Most of the population lives within a 100 miles of the U.S. border, which poses an ongoing concern regarding U.S. economic and cultural domination.

Geography

Canada occupies most of North America and is the world's second-largest country. It has a diverse geography, with mountains, broad prairies, coastal areas, and Arctic ice caps. Canada and the United States share the world's longest border. It has a great number of lakes and a large amount of the world's fresh water. Its northern regions have coniferous forests tapering to tundra and finally to Arctic barrens. The country is rich in minerals, forests, hydroelectric power, and natural gas.

Economy

One of the wealthiest nations in the world, Canada is a free market economy, with slightly more government intervention than in the United States but less than in European countries. It is highly dependent on international trade, especially with the United States.

Types of Investments

There are virtually no restrictions on foreigners buying properties. Canadian housing prices have been rising continuously. Price increases are based on solid economic fundamentals and are not driven by a speculative bubble. Sustained economic growth, income growth, and increased employment have all boosted the demand for housing.

Immigrants play a vital role as renters, especially in Toronto, Vancouver, and Montreal, where more than 70% of the immigrants live. About two-thirds of recent immigrants live in multiple-unit rentals. Yields for apartments are around 9.7% in Toronto.

Who Is Involved in Real Estate Transactions

A license is required to be a real estate broker. Most regions have a listing service similar to that in the United States. For lending purposes, appraisals are not required by law but it is common practice for lenders to request one. Buyers may want to have additional investigations, such as an environmental report, a building inspection, and a zoning review, prepared by a planning consultant. The cost and time needed for these inspections varies.

Sales contracts are similar to those in the United States. Sales contracts do not require notarization or the involvement of an attorney; they can be drawn and executed by a real estate agent. Typically, a standard form is used. Closing of sales and escrow procedures are regulated by the government. Closing and escrow typically last no longer than sixty days from the date of contract for sale but can be longer when purchasing new homes from developers.

Title

Sole ownership, tenancy in common, partnerships, corporations, trusts, and joint ventures are all allowed. Corporate ownership can be either federal or provincial. Federal incorporation takes longer than provincial incorporation and has rather strict financial reporting requirements, but a federally incorporated name is protected throughout Canada. Provincial incorporation, although much quicker than federal, offers protection only within the province.

Adverse possession exists in Canada, but the rights associated with it are quite limited. Adverse possession is established after ten years of uninterrupted and uncontested use of a property.

Taxes and Fees

Costs and taxes for buying properties: about 3% of the value of the
    property (plus 7% Goods and Services Tax (GST) on new and
    renovated houses)

Annual property taxes: levied at the provincial level based on prop-
    erty value

Title transfer: amount varies depending on the province

Realtor commission: 3% to 7%; paid by the seller

Legal fees: shared between buyer and seller

Rental income: Subject to a fixed 25% tax, withheld by the tenant.
    There is another method where you are also taxed at 25%, but cer-
    tain deductions are allowed.

Capital gains: Taxed at both the federal and provincial levels.
    Tax treaty agreements can be applied toward capital gains
    taxes.

Insurance

Insurance is required on mortgages. From time to time, lenders are
written into insurance policies as "co-insureds."

Debt Financing

Loans can be acquired from banks or lending institutions. Property
is held as collateral for a mortgage. There are no statutory restrictions or guidelines that govern the term of loans. Second, third, and
fourth mortgages are allowed.

Inheritance

There is no inheritance or estate tax in Canada. If the surviving
spouse is a resident, he or she acquires the property and capital gains
are deferred. There is no "spousal rollover" for nonresidents. However, if the nonresident is a U.S. resident, the spousal rollover may be
available because of a special provision in the Canada-U.S. Tax Convention.

Foreign Investment Issues

Canada has rather strong tenant protection laws. The initial rent can be freely negotiated between landlord and tenant, except in Prince Edward Islands, where the amount of rent is determined by the Office of the Director of Residential Rental Property. Rents can only be raised once every twelve months in all provinces, with some provinces setting the allowable increase. A landlord cannot evict a tenant for reasons of personal use.

The government has limited eminent domain rights. If a valid public use is demonstrated in the expropriation of private land, the property owner must be compensated at fair market value by means of a valuation analysis. If the owner feels this value is unfair, the value may be appealed judicially. Public zoning requirements are used to safeguard against incompatible land uses in an area and also used to regulate growth. There are also restrictions on the subdivision of real property.

For more information

www.crea.ca

The Canadian Real Estate Association represents more than 88,000 real estate brokers/agents and salespeople working across Canada. Its primary mission is to represent its members at the federal level and to act as a watchdog on national legislation that pertains to the real estate industry.

Mexico

Government

Traditionally, the government has sought to maintain its interests abroad and project its influence largely through moral persuasion. In particular, Mexico champions the principles of nonintervention and self-determination. In its efforts to revitalize its economy and open up to international competition, Mexico has sought closer relations with the United States, Western Europe, and the Pacific Basin. The government will confront continued challenges of boosting economic growth, improving international competitiveness, and reducing poverty.

Society

Spanish is the official language, spoken by nearly everyone. Knowledge of English is increasing rapidly, especially among business people, the middle class, returned emigrants, and the young. Mexico is a predominantly mestizo society (60%); 30% indigenous; 9% European; 1% other. Public education is free and compulsory until age sixteen. The government distributes free textbooks and workbooks to all primary schools.

Geography

Mexico is the third-largest nation in Latin America (after Brazil and Argentina). Massive mountain ranges include the Sierra Madre Occidental to the west, the Sierra Madre Oriental to the east, the Cordillera Neovolcánica in the center of the country, and the Sierra Madre del Sur to the south. Lowlands largely exist along the coasts and in the Yucatán Peninsula, whereas the interior of the country is primarily high plateau. There is frequent seismic activity. Most of the country has two seasons: wet (June through September) and dry (October through April). Generally, there is little rainfall in the interior and to the north, and there is abundant rainfall along the east coast, to the south, and in the Yucatán Peninsula.

Economy

Mexico has a free market economy exceeding $1 trillion. It contains a mixture of modern and outmoded industry and agriculture, increasingly dominated by the private sector. Recent administrations have expanded competition in seaports, railroads, telecommunications, electricity generation, natural gas distribution, and airports.

Income distribution remains highly unequal. Trade with the United States and Canada has tripled since the implementation of the North American Free Trade Agreement in 1994. Mexico has twelve free trade agreements with over forty countries, including Guatemala, Honduras, El Salvador, the European Free Trade Area, and Japan. More than 90% of trade is under free trade agreements.

Who Is Involved in Real Estate Transactions

Registered agents are not required. Notaries handle negotiations and the money. The notary sends the transfer tax to the Treasury Department and applies the applicable tariff based on the state in which the property is located. The notary registers the first testimony of the public deed containing the formalized real estate purchase agreement and the transfer of title at the Public Registry of Property.

Payment Methods

Escrow arrangements generally do not exist in Mexico. It is important to place deposit money with a reputable Mexican or U.S. attorney to be held in a trust account. A bank may also perform this service but charges a setup fee and a commission based on the amount of money held.

Title

All foreign individuals and corporations as well as Mexican corporations that include any foreign investment may hold title to property. However, within restricted zones, title can only be held "indirectly" through a bank trust arrangement known as a *fideicomiso*.

Taxes and Fees

Real estate commissions and fees: 5% to 10%

Legal fees: 2% to 6% of purchase price

Acquisition tax (*Impuesto sobre Adquisiciones o Transmisión de Dominio*): 2%, paid by the buyer

Income tax: 29% on the gain (the excess of the sale price over the adjusted tax basis; paid by seller). The tax basis is the original cost of acquisition updated for inflation. The basis can be shifted in such a manner that the seller owes little or no tax, and the buyer may have a lower basis than what was paid for the property (the buyer inherits the seller's tax basis).

Value-added tax: 15% of transaction price, applicable only to structures (paid by seller). Therefore, an allocation of the price should be made to the land and structures based on an appraisal. Land and residential property are not subject to VAT.

Required Personal Documents

A copy of your passport is required. A copy of the incorporation documentation is required if the purchase is through a corporation.

Buying a Single-Family Dwelling

The following lists the minimum time needed under optimum conditions and the approximate costs to complete the purchase of a dwelling after the offer has been accepted.

	Days	Cost in U.S. $
Obtain the alignment and official number of the property at the corresponding Federal District Department	11	50
Obtain the cadastral from the Cadastre Department at the Public Registry of Property	7	25
Notary obtains a nonencumbrance certificate	7	25
Notary formalizes the purchase agreement	3	18,500
Register the transfer of title at the Public Registry of Property of the Federal District	60	850
Total	88 days	$19,450

Insurance

Some U.S. companies offer title insurance on Mexican real estate interests to non-Mexican investors and lenders. These title policies typically have additional coverage limitations that are not common in the United States, and the cost is also greater. An application fee of at least $3,000 must be paid up front for the lawyer's title search and for copies of the necessary documents. A survey is also required and costs at least $750.

Debt Financing

Mortgage plans are available to low-income families.

Inheritance

The government claims the land if there are no heirs.

Foreign Investment Issues

Zoning and permitting restrictions are relatively tight.

Property can be preempted by tenants or the government if held in good faith for five years and recorded publicly, or even held in bad faith for ten years. With leasehold estates, tenancy is terminated at the will of either party.

For more information

www.ampidf.com.mx
This is the Spanish-language website for the Mexican Association of Real Estate Professionals (AMPI).

Asia/Pacific

Australia

Government
Australia is a federation within a constitutional monarchy using the Westminster parliamentary form as its legislative branch. Australians elect state and territory legislatures. At the national level, elections are held at least once every three years. The prime minister can advise the governor general, who is selected by Queen Elizabeth, to call an election for the House of Representatives at any time. Property rights are well protected, and government expropriation is highly unlikely.

Society
Most of the population is concentrated in the large coastal cities of Sydney, Melbourne, Brisbane, Perth, and Adelaide. Australia has an active tradition of music, ballet, and theater. Many of the performing arts companies receive public funding from the federal government. Education is primarily regulated by the individual state governments. English is the national language. Australia is experiencing a demographic shift toward an older population, with more retirees and fewer people of working age. To boost population growth, it has an active immigration program. Most immigrants are

skilled, and the immigration quota includes categories for family members and refugees.

Geography

Australia has 16,007 miles of coastline. The Great Barrier Reef, the world's largest coral reef, is a short distance off the northeast coast. The world's largest monolith, Mount Augustus, is located in western Australia. Most of Australia is desert or semi-arid. It is the driest inhabited continent and the flattest, and it has the oldest and least fertile soils. Only the southeast and southwest corners of the continent have a temperate climate. The northern part of the country, with a tropical climate, consists of rainforest, woodland, grassland, mangrove swamps, and desert.

Economy

Australia has a prosperous, Western-style mixed economy, with a per capita GDP slightly higher than those of the United Kingdom, Germany, and France in terms of purchasing power parity. The country was ranked third in the United Nations' 2005 Human Development Index and sixth in The Economist's 2005 worldwide quality-of-life index. In recent years, the Australian economy has been resilient in the face of global economic downturn. Rising output in the domestic economy has been offsetting the global slump, and business and consumer confidence remains robust. Tourism remains a primary industry in Australia. Current areas of concern to some economists include Australia's high current account deficit and also the high levels of net foreign debt owed by the private sector.

Types of Investments

A growing number of foreign investors are purchasing property in the major Australian cities and then leasing it to different types of business enterprises. There is also a lot of investment in income-producing real estate involved in the tourism trade. In 2005, the residential vacancy rate was 1.6%. Most investors are from the United States, the United Kingdom, New Zealand, and China.

Who Is Involved in Real Estate Transactions

If you are not an Australian resident, or not entitled to permanent residence, you must obtain approval from the Foreign Investment Review Board. If you purchase property without approval, the property may be subject to a forced sale.

Transactions are conducted by licensed real estate agents, brokers, or auctioneers. Most realtor commissions are paid by the seller, unless the buyer signs a contract with the agent to act as a Buyer's Agent, which then makes the buyer liable for the commission. After an offer is accepted, the buyer places a holding deposit of 10% of the agreed-on price. If either party backs out of the transaction before the contract for sale is completed, the buyer is usually entitled to a refund of the holding deposit. The contract for sale lists all the conditions, restrictions, and requirements prior to closing. Conditions include financing and lien releases. Once the contract of sale is signed, the buyers lose the deposit if they back out, although in some states there is a ten-day rescission or cooling-off period.

Title

Title can be held by individuals, corporations, partnerships, and sole proprietorships. Foreign proprietors must appoint a resident agent who is a resident in the state where the business is registered.

Taxes and Fees

Commission rates: Vary on a sliding scale, increasing according to the value of the property. For example, in Queensland, the state with the lowest maximum, the maximum commission for residential property is 5% of the first $18,000 and 2.5% for the balance of the purchase price.

Residential commission: 1% to 4%

Land sales: 1% to 4%
Commercial: 2% to 3%

Rental income is taxable. You can deduct costs, such as management fees, interest, and depreciation. Australia also has a stamp duty, land tax, and capital gains tax.

Required Personal Documents
A copy of your passport or visa is required.

Buying a Single-Family Dwelling
The following lists the minimum time needed under optimum conditions to complete the purchase of a dwelling after the offer has been accepted.

	Days
File for a title search certificate, maps, and land tax certificate and get recorded easements and covenants from the Land and Property Information Department	1
File for a zoning certificate from the municipal council	2
File for a drainage diagram from the local water authority	1
Obtain ad valorem stamp duty for sales contract at the Office of State Revenue	1
Buyer files notice of sale, transfer, and certificate of title with Land and Property Information	1
Approval of the Foreign Investment Review Board	90
Total	96

Insurance
Financial institutions require that a property be insured.

Debt Financing
Debt financing is available, and there are numerous domestic and foreign banks, as well as building societies and credit unions. There are no government-owned banks.

Inheritance

If the property owner dies within the state and has no survivors, the property is ceded to the government.

For more information

www.reia.com.au/institute/index.asp
The Real Estate Institute of Australia is the national professional association.

www.udia.com.au/html/policy.cfm
The Urban Development Institute of Australia is a federation of five state associations that aims to improve the urban development industry through sustainable urban development.

China

Government

China is an oligarchy consisting of a single party. The regional governments and the army also have a degree of political power. The government has imposed heavy restrictions in some areas, such as the Internet and press. It has mandated population control policies, but environmental policy is lacking. Although China has instituted some environmental regulations, they are disregarded by the local communities for the sake of economic development. Considered a developing nation, China was exempted from the Kyoto Protocol, and since then it has become one of the world's top emitters of carbon gases. The government often resorts to censorship to quell opposition and has a poor international record regarding human rights. China's judicial system is weak, and even when the courts attempt to enforce a decision, local officials ignore the rulings.

Society

China is a multinational country, composed of a large number of ethnic and linguistic groups. The largest group is the Han. Some fifty-five minority groups are spread over approximately three-fifths of the country and have been given some autonomy. In the past decade, the country has become more urbanized, with 80 million to 120 million migrant workers working part-time in the major cities. The literacy rate is very high among youth (ages fifteen to twenty-four). Life expectancy is the third highest in East Asia, after Japan and South Korea.

Geography

China is the one of the largest countries in the world, bordering on fourteen nations. It contains a large variety of landscapes and climates. China's increasing prosperity has also increased damage to the environment. Prolonged drought and poor agricultural practices have caused the desert areas to expand. In general, the environment continues to deteriorate and water pollution has increased because of extensive industrialization, posing one of the most serious threats to the populations. A lot of the drinking water is unsafe, and the cities are experiencing water shortages.

Economy

In 2005, China emerged as the world's third-largest trading nation. The Chinese government reports that the 2005 GDP growth continued at a rate of 9.5%. The standard of living has risen dramatically in recent years. There is a large disparity in wealth between the coastal regions and the remainder of the country.

Types of Investments

To attract more foreign investors, the government has established preferential policies for foreign investment in real estate, effective in 2007. They include exemption from investment tax, allowing foreign investors to obtain funds through various channels and permitting foreign investors to send their profits abroad after paying their taxes. In recent years, the government has encouraged private ownership and expanded bank lending to its citizens, and the investment in residential housing is increasing.

Real estate sales are actually transfers of the right to use land. The government owns the land; individuals only have the right of use. The land user must obtain a certificate for land use signed by the land administration departments at the municipal and county levels. The contract must comply with the requirement of the state's overall urban and rural development and construction plan. The duration of a land use right is determined by the nature of the project. The maximum term is seventy years for residential buildings; fifty years for industrial use; fifty years for the purpose of education, science, technology, health, or sports; forty years for commercial and recreational use and tourism; and fifty years for other uses. Any operational delay can result in the government withdrawing the land use right.

Who Is Involved in Real Estate Transactions

A licensing system for real estate agents and a land auction mechanism are being developed in Shanghai, Beijing, and other cities. China is expected to follow the standards set by the World Trade Organization and other developed countries to assist in the development of a healthy real estate market.

Title

Property ownership is divided into three types:

- Socialist ownership by the people, equivalent to ownership by state
- Collective ownership
- Private ownership by individuals or private entities

Two or more citizens or legal persons can own property. Joint owners have preemptive rights on the same terms and conditions offered third parties.

Taxes and Fees

Any individual or entity that obtains income from state-owned land, buildings, or facilities must pay a land value-added tax. If taxes are not paid, the land and housing administration rejects the title transfer application of the taxpayer. A progressive tax rate is used.

Insurance

The People's Insurance Company of China provides insurance to individuals and collective enterprises. Foreign insurance firms have representative offices in China, and the Chinese have entered some offshore joint ventures with foreign firms.

Debt Financing

Shenzhen and Guangdong provinces have enacted legislation to provide procedures for mortgages on real property. Mortgage agreements must be notarized and registered with the city land bureau. The dominant banking institutions are four state-owned banks.

Inheritance

Parents, spouses, and children have a right to inherit each other's property. Inheritance law is based on intestate succession and by will.

For more information

www.ccdpc.org.cn
The China Real Estate Association website is in Chinese.

Hong Kong

Government

Hong Kong is part of the People's Republic of China, although it remains a separate economic system. It was a British colony for 130 years until the 1997 transfer of sovereignty to China. The agreement between the United Kingdom and China stipulates that Hong Kong will operate with a high degree of autonomy until at least 2047. A major gateway to the Chinese economy, Hong Kong maintains its own legal system, police force, monetary system, and customs policy. Governance of Hong Kong is run as a special administrative region (SAR), headed by a chief executive.

Society

Most of the population is of Chinese descent, the majority from Guangdong province and from Hong Kong itself. Chinese and English are both official languages. Chinese, especially Cantonese in the spoken form, is the common language. The use of Mandarin Chinese is rising as Hong Kong reintegrates with China. The educational system has roughly followed the British system. Hong Kong is frequently described as a city where East meets West. The influences of British rule can be seen in street signs, dress, and cultural interests while coexisting with traditional philosophies and practices of China.

Geography

Comprising over 260 islands, Hong Kong is located on the banks of the Pearl River Delta, where the area is flat. Other parts of the territory are quite rugged and undeveloped. Despite its reputation of being intensely urbanized, Hong Kong has been called one of the greenest cities in Asia. Less than 25% is developed, and 40% is reserved as parks and nature reserves. Environmental awareness is growing as its air ranks as one of the most polluted. The climate is subtropical and prone to monsoons.

Economy

The vast bulk of Hong Kong's economy is built on the service sector as a corporate and financial center, with the greatest concentration of corporate headquarters in the region. It has one of the highest GDPs per capita in Asia. Because Hong Kong has little arable land and few natural resources, it must import most of its food and raw materials. Tax rates are among the lowest in the world. Under a dual income tax system, individuals are taxed either progressively, between 2% and 19%, on income adjusted for deductions and allowances or at a flat rate of 16% on their gross income, depending on which liability is lower. The top income tax rate is 17.5%. The estate (inheritance) tax was abolished in 2006.

Types of Investments

Foreigners can generally buy properties such as apartments and condominiums and rent them out without restriction. However, residents of some countries, including mainland China (unless they are permanent residents in another country), cannot buy property in Hong Kong. In 2006, because of stagnation, prices for small apartments dropped slightly, but luxury apartments held their value. The Hong Kong residential market is somewhat unusual in that returns on higher-end residential properties are consistently better than those on lower-end properties. Higher-end properties, however, are more volatile in pricing. Rents can be freely negotiated in the private sector, which comprises about half of the rental market.

Buying land is a different story. St. John's Cathedral is the only freehold property in Hong Kong. All other land belongs to the government, and land tenure is on a renewable leasehold basis. Land leases have in the past been granted for 75, 99, or 999 years, and at present are being granted for 50 years. The government has taken a more active role in shaping land use through aggressive planning and zoning. Although deed restrictions are rare, government regulations on land use do exist. Condominiums are permitted, but keep in mind that the land is leased from the SAR and ultimately from China.

Who Is Involved in Real Estate Transactions

Real estate agencies must be licensed and comply with the appropriate regulations. Open listings are not available. Information on pricing is primarily obtained from local contacts, not official records. Funding the purchase is done through legal counsel. There is no escrow service. Hong Kong contract law is very similar to U.S. law, as both are based on English common law.

Title

Ownership is actually a leasehold, and a deed is granted upon conveyance. Land is held by deed rather than by title and is leased from the government. Land may be conveyed, subject to government lease, by inheritance. Frequently, however, the original land lessee will lease land to a developer rather than sell because of its high value as a result of the scarcity of buildable land. The government can condemn and take land for the public good. Ownership can be individual, corporate, limited partnership, tenancy in common, joint tenancy, joint venture, and trust.

Taxes and Fees

Commissions: 1% of the gross sale price; paid by the seller. If the buyer is represented, the fee may be split.

Stamp duty: up to 2.75% on all property transactions, typically split between the buyer and seller

Legal fees: about 1%

Net property income: Taxed at 16%. Net income is computed by deducting a standard 20% for repairs and expenses.

Hong Kong has no capital gains tax or inheritance tax.

Insurance

Fire and casualty insurance are available.

Debt Financing

Mortgage practices are similar to those in the United States. Lending sources consist of banks and seller financing. Sellers frequently provide the financing in the form of a purchase money mortgage.

For more information

www.eaa.org.hk

Estate Agents Authority (EAA) promotes industry standards for estate agents in Hong Kong, provides a complaint forum, and enhances protection for consumers.

www.gpa.gov.hk

The Government Property Agency manages government-owned properties that are available for lease. Information on the various properties is listed.

www.landreg.gov.hk

Land Registry of the Hong Kong SAR allows you to search land records and register deeds.

Japan

Government

Although Japan is a constitutional monarchy, the emperor has very limited power and functions mostly in a ceremonial capacity. Power is held chiefly by the prime minister and other elected members of the Diet, a bicameral parliament. Although the prime minister is theoretically very powerful, the position is weakened by the factional nature of Japanese politics and the tendency toward coalition government. The liberal-conservative Liberal Democratic Party (LDP) has been in power since 1955, except for a short-lived coalition government formed from opposition parties in 1993.

Japan maintains close economic and military relations with its key ally the United States. Currently serving as a nonpermanent Security Council member, Japan is seeking permanent membership. The country actively participates in international affairs and is the second-largest donor of development assistance. Japan has several territorial disputes with its neighbors, Russia, South Korea,

China, and Taiwan, which in part are about control of marine and natural resources, such as possible reserves of crude oil and natural gas.

Society

For the most part, Japanese society is linguistically and culturally homogeneous, with only small populations of foreign workers. Japan has one of the highest life expectancy rates in the world. However, the population is rapidly aging because of a decrease in births in the latter part of the twentieth century. This is creating a potential decline in the workforce population and an increase in costs for social security benefits. The government offers universal health care. A majority of the population profess to believe in both Shinto, the indigenous religion of Japan, and Buddhism. Not one religion is dominant, and each is affected by the other. It is typical for one person or family to believe in several Shinto gods and at the same time belong to a Buddhist sect. Japan is an extremely urban society, with only about 5% of the labor force engaged in agriculture.

Geography

Japan is a country of over 3,000 islands, with more than two-thirds forested, mountainous, and unsuitable for agricultural, industrial, or residential use. This is due to steep elevations, the climate, and the risk of landslides caused by earthquakes or heavy rain. As a result, most of the population lives in the coastal areas. Japan experiences frequent low-intensity tremors and occasional volcanic activity. Destructive earthquakes, often resulting in tsunamis, occur several times each century. There are numerous hot springs, which have been developed into resorts. As a result of a number of environmental disasters, Japan has developed regulations to reduce pollution, preserve endangered species, and minimize the destruction of the environment. The United Nations convention on climate change took place in Kyoto in 1997.

Economy

Japan is one of the world's most developed countries, with a high standard of living. Close government-industry cooperation, a strong work ethic, mastery of high technology, and a comparatively small defense budget, have helped make Japan the second-largest economy in the world, after the United States, in terms of GDP. After World War II, it achieved rapid economic growth by pursuing an aggressive export-oriented economic policy, but high levels of protectionism left the country vulnerable. The economy experienced a severe recession in the early 1990s, largely due to overinvestment. Long-term challenges include an immense government debt equaling 170% of the GDP and a rapidly aging population combined with low birth rates.

The service sector accounts for about three-quarters of the economic output. Japan is home to large financial service companies as well as several multinational companies. A recent bill to privatize the postal system, the world's largest financial institution, which controls about US$3.35 trillion of personal savings and insurance funds, was passed. The decision to privatize has been a contentious political battle.

Types of Investments

Despite the economic contraction, the housing market is still quite a good investment because house prices have been falling faster than rents, leading to higher yields. The gross rental yield for properties in Tokyo ranges from 4.5% to 8%. This is high for a country where interest rates are near zero and deflation is the norm. As more and more people move to the city, the rental market remains robust. Between 1995 to 2005, rents fell by 11.4% nationwide and by 10.7% in Tokyo. Over the same period, residential land prices fell by 32% overall in Japan and 40% in Tokyo.

No property rights can be created other than those provided for in Civil Code or other laws. Laws set zoning designations for every plot of land, which determine how much of the land may be used for a building and the size and kind of building that may be erected. One factor affecting any property development, for example, is the width of the road that borders it. The height of a building is figured as a percentage of road width, and the higher floors are often set back from the road's edge in compulsory setback lines.

Tenancy laws passed in 2000 shifted the balance of power from tenants to landlords, making Japan strongly pro-landlord. Rents are freely negotiable, and leases are not automatically renewed when the contract expires.

Who Is Involved in Real Estate Transactions

A license is not required to engage in brokerage business. Real estate brokers only market properties and are not involved in drafting contracts. Real estate contracts are generally prepared by either the seller or an attorney. Standard forms of contracts are governed by the Civil Code. Provisions can be modified by agreement of the parties involved.

Title

Ownership is determined from registration records. Sole ownership is the most commonly held method. Title can also be tenancy in common. Partnership arrangements are not known; however, partnership corporations and informal associations (*Kumiai*) have many features similar to partnerships. Joint stock corporation is the most common in business circles and most closely resembles a U.S. corporation. It is not necessary to record a title to make it valid. However, it should be registered to make the transfer public and is required for obtaining a mortgage.

Taxes and Fees

Broker commission: Based on a percentage of the transaction; paid by the buyer and seller equally. When properties are rented, the tenant, not the landlord, pays the broker a fee equal to one month's rent.

Legal fees: varies

Transfer tax: none

Rental income: Gross rental income of nonresidents subject to 20% withholding tax. Real estate taxes are imposed by municipalities on the assessed value of the land or building.

Capital gains: 30% for property held for less than five years. Beyond five years, it is taxed at 10% to 20%, depending on the value.

Income tax: Permanent residents are taxed on worldwide income.

Debt Financing

In most instances, local financing is available to foreign investors on the same basis as it is to domestic companies. Loans from financial institutions usually require some form of tangible or financial collateral or guarantees from the parent company. The four chief methods of financing commercial real estate in Japan are business loans, key money deposits of tenants, joint ventures, and real estate security sales.

Mortgage financing is seldom done on a direct basis. The credit standing of the company or the individual is the first and most important consideration, and collateral is usually a secondary consideration. The lender may accept the real estate as an auxiliary form of collateral (one of the reasons is that it is difficult to foreclose on an income property because of tenant rights). Therefore, most loans for real estate acquisition as well as development are commercial loans. "Key money" refers to money that is paid by the tenant to the owner of the property for the privilege of signing a contract. Key money deposits are often paid on a square meter basis in addition to regular security deposits. Industrial property is usually financed through the issuance and sale of corporate securities by the industrial company needing the industrial premises. In Japan, companies rarely lease the premises.

Inheritance

Inheritance tax is based on the residence status of the individual. There is no inheritance tax for foreigners, but a registration fee must be paid to transfer title at 0.2% of the property value. Nonresidents may still be subject to inheritance tax if they have been residents in Japan at any time within five years before the deceased's death. Inheritance tax is levied at progressive rates on the fair market value of the property inherited, less funeral expenses and taxes.

For more information
www.homenavi.or.jp/english/profile.htm
The Association of Real Estate Agents of Japan is a member organization that provides information and promotes industry standards. It lists available properties and contacts to agents that speak English.

New Zealand

Government
New Zealand is a constitutional monarchy with a parliamentary democracy. Elizabeth II, as the queen of New Zealand, is the head of state but has no real political influence. Political power is held by the democratically elected parliament under the leadership of the prime minister. The New Zealand Nuclear Free Zone Act of 1987 prohibits nuclear arms or nuclear-propelled ships from entering its waters. This legislation has been a source of contention with the United States and is the basis for the U.S. suspension of treaty obligations with New Zealand.

Society
The population is mostly of European descent, with the indigenous Maori being the largest minority. Non-Maori Polynesian and Asians are also significant minorities, especially in the cities. As part of increasing the country's population, New Zealand has a relatively open immigration policy. Over 20% of the population was born overseas, one of the highest rates in the world. Both English and Maori are the official languages.

Geography

New Zealand comprises two main islands and a number of smaller islands. It has a dramatic and varied landscape, with extensive marine resources. The country is geographically isolated, with Australia being about 1,250 miles to the northwest. The climate throughout the country is mild, mostly cool temperate to warm temperate. Because of its geographic isolation, New Zealand has unique flora and fauna. About 80% of the flora exist only in New Zealand. To ensure survival of its unique native species, the country has programs to prevent nonnative species from being introduced.

Economy

New Zealand has a modern developed economy with a high standard of living. The country is heavily dependent on trade, especially in agriculture, which constitutes about 28% of its exports, making it vulnerable to global economic slowdowns. After experiencing economic slumps in the last decades of the twentieth century, the country has rebound, enjoying a substantial economic boom. In the 1980s, many of the government-owned enterprises were privatized.

Types of Investments

Investors from all over the world are focusing on Auckland because of its large increase in population. The Auckland City Council is dedicated to significantly increasing the density of housing. Nonresidents can buy property under NZ$50 million and land under five hectares without requiring consent from the New Zealand government. Common investments are apartment buildings, developments, and commercial real estate. Currently, demand is very high, and properties are on the market for a very short time, but this may change with the recent increase of interest rates. New Zealand encourages foreign investment, and barriers to investment are minimal.

Traditional tribal boundaries, called "rohe," are still recognized.

The rohe are often defined according to prominent geographical features, such as mountains, rivers, and lakes. Purchases of farm land, environmentally sensitive lands, areas deemed historic or culturally significant, and offshore islands require prior consent by the land valuation tribunal.

Who Is Involved in Real Estate Transactions

Solicitors often prepare or review contracts. Contract law is similar to that of England. Contracts for the sale of real property do not need to be notarized. Closings typically occur within sixty days of contract execution.

Real estate agents prepare tenancy documentation, and standard residential tenancy forms are used for residential property. In the case of commercial leases, the preliminary Agreement to Lease is prepared by the agent. After signing the Agreement to Lease, the formal Deeds of Lease is prepared by the owner's solicitor.

Payment Methods

Generally, 10% is held in a trust account by the buyer's solicitor. Any interest earned on the funds is either split equally at settlement or goes fully to the buyer.

Title

One or more individuals, corporations, partnerships, joint ventures, or a trust can own property. Spouses can hold title to property separately. The primary residence of a husband and wife is considered community property with the right of survivorship upon the death of either spouse.

Partnerships cannot exceed twenty-five partners. "Special Partnerships" are similar to limited partnerships in that the special partners are not responsible for debts of the partnership. Each special partnership must have at least one general partner.

There is no need for title insurance under the Government Land Registry.

Tax and Fees

Real estate commissions: 3% to 4% of the selling price, paid by the
  seller
Agents fees: 2% to 3%
Legal fees: NZ$800 to NZ$1,000
Loan application (if borrowing funds): NZ$350
Valuation fee (if borrowing funds): NZ$350
Pre-settlement inspection: NZ$350
Capital gains: Properties held for long term are not subject to capi-
  tal gains.

Required Personal Documents

A copy of your passport is required.

Debt Financing

Fixed-rate loans of greater than 60% of value and terms in excess of ten
years are common. Banks and institutions provide mortgage financing.

Inheritance

Real property can be conveyed after death via a written will. If the
owner dies with no survivors, the property is transferred to the government. There is no inheritance tax or duty in New Zealand.

Foreign Investment Issues

There are no restrictions on transfers, repatriation of profits, or access to foreign exchange. Title to property can be gained through adverse possession if the property is used uninterruptedly for at least
twenty years.

For more information

www.reinz.co.nz
The Real Estate Institute of New Zealand (REINZ) offers information on market trends, advice on buying and selling, and contact information for local realtors.

www.realestate.co.nz

This website offers an extensive list of properties for sale, including rural, residential, and commercial. All properties are listed by a licensed member of the REINZ.

Europe

Austria

Government
Austria is a republic. The current government has successfully pursued a comprehensive economic reform program aimed at streamlining government; creating a more competitive business environment, further strengthening Austria's attractiveness as an investment location; pursuing a balanced budget; and implementing effective pension reforms.

Society
Roughly 90% of the population are German-speaking Austrians. The rest of the population is mostly from surrounding countries, especially the former Soviet Union and Yugoslavia. It is predominately a Roman Catholic country.

Geography
Austria is a small, landlocked, predominantly mountainous country. Temperatures and rainfall vary with altitude. As a result of domestic and foreign pollution, 37% of its forests have been damaged by acid rain and/or pollutant emissions. The damage has had dire consequences, because the forests had protected many Alpine communities from avalanches, erosion, mud slides, and flooding caused by runoff.

Economy

Austria, with its well-developed market economy and high standard of living, is closely tied to other EU economies, especially Germany's. The economy also benefits greatly from strong commercial relations, especially in the banking and insurance sectors, with central, eastern, and southeastern Europe. The economy features a large service sector, a sound industrial sector, and a small but highly developed agricultural sector. Membership in the EU has drawn an influx of foreign investors. Weak domestic consumption and slow growth in Europe have held the economy to growth rates of less than 2.5% as of 2006.

Types of Investments

The majority of foreign nationals purchasing single-family residences is German, with Southern Tyrolean and other Italians second. Most purchases are for second homes, which are often rented or leased to third parties. Most real estate experts believe that vacation rentals will continue well into the future. The state land control board must approve land purchases by foreign individuals or companies. Property costs tend to run far higher than in other countries around the world.

The Austrian government retains certain rights in real property, such as the right to levy property taxes, the right of escheat, and the right to control the use of private property through zoning. The legal system protects secured interests in real property.

Who Is Involved in Real Estate Transactions

Approximately 35% of all real estate transactions involve agents. At the time the purchase agreement is executed, the buyer posts a 10% deposit, which is held in escrow pending the completion of the sales transaction. If the sale falls apart through no fault of the buyer, the deposit is returned.

Any transfers of property must be entered with the land registry, but before being filed, either the land transfer commission or the office of the provincial governor must approve the transfer. Mortgage information is also kept on file with the land registry. Registering real estate with the land registry can take up to three or four months.

Title

Corporations and partnerships may acquire, hold, and convey title to real property.

There is no state guarantee of title. Generally, a bona fide third party can rely on the correctness and completeness of the recording in the land title register. Real estate law is governed by the principle that earlier rights trump later rights. Prior registered rights have priority over subsequent registered rights, and registered rights prevail over unregistered rights. To secure the buyer's position, the seller may request a court-issued order of precedence for acquisition. The order of precedence is registered and is granted for up to one year, during which the buyer may request the registration of his right in the earlier rank of the order of precedence, superseding registrations of a later rank.

Taxes and Fees

Sales commissions: 3% to 5% for residential sales and slightly lower for commercial transactions; typically paid by the seller

Notary fee: 1%

Registration fee: 4.5%

Transfer tax: 3.5%

Capital gains tax: Homeowners who have maintained residence in a property for at least two years are not subject to capital gains tax on its sale.

Ad valorem land tax: Levied based on the standard tax value of the property. This tax is approximately 0.8% but may vary according to jurisdiction. Additionally, a land value tax of approximately 1% may be levied on vacant land.

Debt Financing

Real property can be mortgaged as security for a debt in Austria. Mortgage deeds must state the exact amount and must be filed with the land registry. Priority of mortgages depends on their date of registration. Austria has a highly developed banking system with worldwide relationships, as well as representative offices and branches in the United States and other major financial centers.

For more information

www.ovi.at

This German-language website provides information for those involved in the real estate profession in Austria.

Bulgaria

Government

Bulgaria was under Soviet influence after World War II until 1989 with the collapse of the Soviet Union. Bulgaria is now a parliamentary democracy in which the prime minister occupies the most powerful executive position. It became a member of the European Union in January 2007. Despite a dramatic increase in foreign ownership of land, the legal system remains largely ineffective, allowing organized crime and corruption to hamper investment. Although necessary legal changes are unlikely until the next round of parliamentary elections, the new parliament will face greater pressure from the EU to proceed more vigorously with legal reforms.

Society

The majority of the population is ethnic Bulgarian; about 10% are Turks and 5% are Roma. Most Bulgarians are members of the Bulgarian Orthodox Church; 12% are Muslim. Bulgaria's literacy rate is 98.6%. It has one of the lowest birth rates and has had a negative growth in population since the 1990s.

Geography

Bulgaria is located in southeastern Europe. Considering its relatively small size, Bulgaria has substantial climatic variation because it is located at the meeting point of Mediterranean and continental air masses and because its mountains partition climatic zones. Its beach resorts are popular with tourists from other European countries.

Economy

Economic difficulties and a tide of corruption led over 800,000 Bulgarians, most of them qualified professionals, to emigrate. With international support, Bulgaria adopted a broad reform program in 1997 that included major trade and price liberalization, social-sector reform, establishment of a currency board, restructuring of all sectors, and divestiture of state-owned enterprises. The program transformed Bulgaria's economy, lowered inflation, and improved investor confidence.

Economic policy continues to focus on commitments to International Monetary Fund guidelines and EU entry requirements. Despite tensions about the privatization of certain key industries, the government has progressed significantly in its economic reforms through 2006.

Types of Investments

Parliament changed the constitution to permit foreign ownership of land, provided the owners are from EU countries or countries with an international agreement permitting such purchases. Because of the prohibitions against foreign ownership of land, many people opt to purchase apartments. Apartments normally are sold as units without the conveyance of any actual land, so a foreigner may purchase and own an apartment. Apartment sales have been brisk; many buying vacation apartments in the Black Sea resorts. There is a trend toward the rehabilitation of older properties. Since the late 1990s, Bulgaria has worked diligently to attract tourists and tourism money.

Who Is Involved in Real Estate Transactions

There are no license requirements needed to sell property. The activities of notaries public at regional courts include certifying signatures and copies of documents and drawing up formal declarations and documents, mortgages, wills, acts related to reincorporation of companies, and transfers of real property. Fees are regulated by law and increase according to the amount involved in the transaction.

A 10% to 20% deposit holds the property for a specified amount of time as agreed in the contract. Sales involving real property must be in the form of a notarized deed. To be a valid contract, it must have mutual consent and a description of the property, and both the buyer and seller must be competent. Appraisals are done by both individuals and businesses. Appraisals are similar to those performed in the United States, but they are much less detailed.

Payment Methods

Transferring money can take three to ten days, and the Bulgarian bank may need another three days to access the funds. The notary executes the transfer deed and collects the money for payment of the transfer tax and registration fee. This is done for the clients' convenience. The parties can pay the fees themselves directly to the tax authority and bring the receipts to the notary.

Required Personal Documents

A copy of your passport, local identification, or birth certificate is required.

Title

Foreigners purchasing land must establish a Bulgarian Limited Company to purchase and own the land. It costs about €1,000 to set up and, in most instances, a qualified real estate agent can do it.

Tax and Fees

Commissions: 1.5% to 3%, paid by both seller and buyer (negotiated and not mandated by law)

Transfer tax: 2% of the property price

Registration fee: 0.1% of the price

Municipal fees: 2% of market value

Property tax: 0.15% of the property's list value

VAT: 20% payable on all real estate transactions, except when the property is for residential use

Capital gains tax: none

Debt Financing

Mortgages are based on the entire real estate property and its accessories. The maximum loan is 70% of the property value. Loans are based on your net income. All your existing liabilities, including any mortgage/rent payments, personal bank loans, credit card payments, and so on, together with your proposed mortgage payment, must not exceed 40% of your net monthly income.

For more information

www.nsni.bg/eng_index1.aspx

The National Real Property Association promotes the real estate industry by establishing industry standards. Its website contains some information about foreigners buying real estate.

www.adis.bg/en

ADIS is a full-service agency with multiple listings.

France

Government

France is a republic. French politics have been characterized by two politically opposed groupings: one left-wing, centered on the

French Socialist Party, and the other right-wing, centered on the Union pour un Mouvement Populaire (UMP). French foreign policy has been largely shaped by membership in the European Union.

Society

France is one of the most diverse countries in Europe with about 56% of the population of foreign background. The French healthcare system has been ranked number one in the world by the World Health Organization. France is predominantly a Roman Catholic country, but it is very secular. Freedom of religion is constitutionally a right. Tensions erupt because of discrimination against minorities.

Geography

France's landscapes are extremely varied from one region to another, ranging from high alpine territory to oceanfront resort towns.

Economy

Growth is sluggish, and the unemployment rate is persistently high. The government has reduced the long-term unemployment benefit period for workers under age fifty from three years to two and has weakened the thirty-five-hour workweek mandate by allowing employers to offer workers a higher rate of pay for additional hours.

Types of Investments

Foreign investors in commercial real estate, particularly in buildings and property associated with retail operations, have doubled in recent years. The commercial real estate market in major French cities is a profitable investment and should remain so for years to come. Many foreign nationals have been purchasing residences in rural areas and in large French cities. For many years, France has been a destination of choice for vacationers.

Who Is Involved in Real Estate Transactions

All transactions involve a notaire, but real estate brokers can be used to locate property. The contract of sale may be made by notarial deed or in the form of a private agreement. The promise to sell or buy real estate is void if not contained in a notarized or private act registered at the tax registry office within ten days after acceptance by the buyer. It takes about six months to acquire a property.

Payment Methods

The notaire holds the deposits and payment until all of the requirements and obligations of the sales contract have been completed. At that time, the money is paid to the seller.

Title

Title may be held as individuals and other entities.

Taxes and Fees

Transaction costs: 6% to 7% of the value to the notaire

Stamp duty: 19% of the value, and 18.6% brokerage fees if a broker is used

Property taxes: Determined annually; 50% of the value is taxed at the applicable rate. Individuals who occupy a furnished dwelling are subject to a residence tax, whether they own or rent the property. The tax is calculated by applying the local rate to the annual rental value as indicated in the land records.

Capital gains tax: 33.33%; generous tax breaks are available to investors who buy into freehold residential tourist hot spots

Insurance

Most lenders require life insurance for individual owners with a mortgage over €250,000.

Debt Financing

Banks lend based on the income and expense of the purchaser. Loan-to-value (LTV) ratios vary widely, from 50% to 100%. Non-EU citizens may not exceed an 85% LTV. The maximum mortgage term is thirty-five years.

When applying for a mortgage, you need your last three salary pay statements or pension vouchers and your last tax return. If you are an employer or are self-employed, you need your tax returns and annual accounts for the last two or three fiscal years, as well as extensive information about other fully or partly owned properties, including profit and loss statements.

Inheritance

Only French assets are liable to estate taxes. Taxable assets include properties, tangible assets, and shares in French companies. French succession law applies to properties in France, even if the owners are not French nationals. Under French succession law, you are not able to leave your assets to anyone you please. Children come first, and your spouse or partner is treated very differently. You should take advice from your notaire and act on it before signing the sales agreement. It is difficult to make changes once the sales agreement has been registered, and this can cause serious consequences.

Preemption Rights

The commune where the property is situated can preempt the property if it is needed for development purposes. A tenant also has the right of preemption when the owner sells occupied premises for the purpose of dividing it into a condominium. In this situation, the owner sends a notification to the tenant who has one month to reply. If the tenant wishes to buy the property, the tenant has two months to complete the purchase or four months if the tenant requires a loan.

If the owner sells the property without notifying the tenant or sells at a lower price than that offered to the tenant, the tenant can take priority over the purchaser within one month following completion.

In rural areas, farmers and the Agricultural Commission both have a right of preemption over land or property.

For more information
http://realestate.meetup.com/216
Paris Real Estate Buying & Investing Network exchanges information on buying property in France.

Spain

Government
Spain is a constitutional monarchy and is widely regarded as the most decentralized state in Europe. Territories manage their own health and educational systems, and some also manage their own public finances without interference from the Spanish central government. The government has a long-running campaign against the ETA, a Basque liberation movement that at times has used violent means.

Society
An estimated 4.8 million foreigners, about 11% of the population, live in Spain. Spain currently is thought to have one of the highest immigration rates within the EU. This is a result of its geographic position, the porosity of its borders, the large size of its underground economy, and the strength of the agricultural and construction sectors, which demand more low-cost labor than can be offered by the national workforce. Roman Catholicism is the most common religion in the country. Its educational system is considered one of the weakest in Europe.

Geography
Spain is dominated by high plateaus and mountain ranges such as the Pyrenees. It is bound to the south and east by the Mediterranean Sea, to the north by the Bay of Biscay, and to the west by the

Atlantic Ocean. Spain's Canary Islands are off the coast of Africa. Spain's climate is extremely diverse.

Economy

Spain's mixed economy supports a GDP that on a per capita basis is 87% of that of the four leading West European economies. Lately, the country has attracted significant amounts of foreign investment. Tourism is one of the leading industries. The 2006 government has plans to reduce government intervention in business, combat tax fraud, and support innovation, research and development, but it also intends to reintroduce labor market regulations. The country has had a real estate boom but increasing prices have also increased the levels of personal debt.

Types of Investments

There are 1.1 million non-Spanish property owners. Most are from United Kingdom, the Middle East, Germany, and Scandinavia.

Who Is Involved in Real Estate Transactions

Transactions can involve agents, attorneys, notaries, and CPAs. There are many types of contracts recognized under Spanish law. In general, a valid contract contains price, property description, and term of execution.

Payment Methods

Some agents establish trust accounts and manage third-party funds that are held until the contract conditions are met. Currently, no bonds or errors and omissions insurance is available to protect these funds. Some companies in the country have established escrow services as third-party neutral agents, and some U.S. title insurance companies are now offering escrow services through their U.S.-based escrow accounts when used in conjunction with the issuance of title insurance.

Title

Title may be held by personal ownership, corporations, partnerships, joint ventures, sole proprietorships, and limited liability companies.

Taxes and Fees

Sales commissions: 3% to 5%

Commissions on leases: 10%

Registration fee: 6.5%

Stamp duty: 0.5%

Rental income: 25% of gross rents without any deductions

Ad valorem tax: 0.3% for rural property and 0.4% for urban property, although each municipality may increase the tax rates of its jurisdiction up to certain limits

Required Personal Documents

A copy of your passport is required. Proof of marital status is also required.

Debt Financing

Real estate can be mortgaged. The mortgage must be executed in a public deed before a notary and entered in the Registry of Deeds. Mortgages automatically expire after twenty years, unless renewed. To apply for a mortgage, you need your last three salary pay statements or pension vouchers and last income tax return. If you are an employer or are self-employed, you need tax returns and income statements for the last two fiscal years. You also need details about the property, a curriculum vitae, and a statement of other income, investments, debts, and properties whether abroad or in Spain.

Inheritance

Inheritance tax is levied on the inheritance of assets, regardless of residency, and the rates are based on the relationship of the beneficiaries to the deceased.

Foreign Investment Issues

In 2007, Spain made significant changes to its taxation system. One beneficial change is the lowering of the capital gains tax for nonresidents selling property. Previously, foreign owners paid 35%, as compared with residents, who pay 18%. The change was brought about by pressure from the European Commission, which seeks taxation harmony in the EU and viewed the difference as discriminatory.

However, other changes certainly make it less attractive to buy property in Spain through either an offshore or an onshore company structure. Previously, investors who bought and flipped real estate could reduce their tax burden through the use of an onshore asset holding company. With the new regulations, the tax rate for these companies rises to between 25% and 30%. For those who own property in this way, the government is allowing a transition period during which time they can close the company and acquire the property assets in their own name. Offshore companies whose primary assets are Spanish real estate will now be considered resident in Spain and taxed accordingly. Therefore, it makes little or no sense to go this route when buying.

Preemption Rights

If a landlord sells occupied property during the life of a rental contract, the tenant has the right of preemption. The owner must first offer to sell the property to the tenant, who has thirty days to reply. If the landlord does not make this offer, or the property is sold at a lower price than the offered one, the tenant could, within one month following completion, have the sale annulled and purchase the property for the price declared in the sales document. A preemption right renunciation agreement is valid for rental contracts that exceed five years.

The Spanish government can control private property through zoning and the application of police power.

For more information
www.consejocoapis.org
This is the Spanish-language website for Spain's professional organization for real estate agents.

United Kingdom

Government
The United Kingdom is a constitutional monarchy and a parliamentary democracy. The country's head of state is the reigning king or queen, and the head of government is the prime minister, who is the leader of the majority political party in the House of Commons. The UK is made up of four countries: England, Scotland, Wales, and Northern Ireland. It also has overseas territories. The UK is very influential in world politics. It is a founding member of NATO and the United Nations, where it holds permanent membership. It is a major military power.

Society
The UK is one of the most densely populated nations in the world. For centuries people have migrated to the British Isles from many parts of the world, some to avoid political or religious persecution, others to find a better way of life or to escape poverty. After 1945, large numbers of other European refugees settled in the country. The large immigrant communities from the West Indies, South Asia, and other parts of the former British Empire date from the 1950s and 1960s. There are also substantial groups of Americans, Australians, and Chinese, as well as various other Europeans. People of Indian, Pakistani, and Bangladeshi origin account for more than half of the total ethnic minority population, and people of West Indian origin are the next largest group. Most immigrants are concentrated in inner-city areas, and more than half live around London.

Geography

The physical geography varies greatly. The climate is generally temperate, with rainfall ranging from 22 to 120 inches per year in different parts of the country. Even areas with lower rainfall may experience rain more than 100 days per year. Agriculture is intensive, with most farmland used as pastures. The UK has large coal, natural gas, and oil reserves. The UK is reducing greenhouse gas emissions and participates in the Kyoto Protocol.

Economy

The United Kingdom, particularly London, has traditionally been a world financial center. Restructuring and deregulation transformed the sector during the 1980s and 1990s, with important changes in banking, insurance, the London Stock Exchange, shipping, and commodity markets. Some long-standing distinctions between financial institutions have become less clear-cut. For example, housing loans used to be primarily the responsibility of building societies, but increasingly banks and insurance companies have entered this area of lending. Two related developments have occurred: the transformation of building-society branch offices into virtual banks with personal cashing facilities and the diversification of all three of these types of institutions into real estate services. Building societies also participate to a limited extent in investment services, insurance, trusteeship, executorship, and land services.

Types of Investments

There are no restrictions on foreign ownership of property. The housing-price boom of the 1990s is slowing, but prices are leveling off much more gently than most analysts had foreseen. Most analysts expect the price slowdown to continue. Rental yields on houses in the UK are now slightly higher than yields on flats, probably reflecting the effects of the decade-long increases in investment in buy-to-let flats. Rents across the country appear to be on a long-term uptrend.

Who Is Involved in Real Estate Transactions

Real estate agents are not required to have a license to conduct real estate transactions. The role of a buyer's agent is not commonplace, although this may change with the government's reform of the home buying and selling process. Multilisting is not common practice, with many agencies having exclusive listings or sole selling rights. This has led to the development of two other types of agencies: the multiple agency, where more than one agent may be instructed by a seller, and the subagency, where a sole selling agent may, with the seller's authority, invite selected agents to act in a subagency capacity. In those circumstances, payment of fees lies between the subagent and the head agent.

A conveyancer is responsible for handling the movement of funds. A 10% deposit is paid to the seller's conveyancer on exchange of contracts. The transfer of funds on completion is handled by the buyer's conveyancer and the seller's conveyancer.

Future changes proposed by the government may see estate agents becoming more responsible for the preparation of presale information coupled with the growth of home inspectors to provide reports as part of the initial information available to home buyers.

Title

Title may be held as sole ownership, tenancy in common, and trust. There is no restriction on the number of individuals who may hold land. The buyer must complete, sign, and post a Land Transaction Return with the Inland Revenue within thirty days of completion together with the stamp duty land tax. The return must be accompanied by payment of the correct amount of tax.

Taxes and Fees

Capital gains tax: Profits from a sale are taxed according to income tax rates, unless you are selling your primary residence.

Withholding tax or rental income: A flat rate of 22% must be withheld by the tenant or letting agent, if there is one, unless other arrangements are made to receive rent untaxed and pay tax later.

Council tax: Annual local tax, based on the property value. There is one council tax bill for each dwelling, whether it is owned or rented. Property owners are the persons usually liable for this tax, except in cases of assured tenancy when the tenant pays the tax.

Debt Financing

There are well over a hundred lenders either in the form of banks or building societies, the latter operating on a mutual basis for the benefit of borrowers and investors. Mortgage fees have risen substantially as interest rates have begun to increase.

Inheritance

Transfer of assets during a taxpayer's lifetime or death is subject to inheritance tax. Estates or assets exceeding the current tax threshold are taxable at a rate of 40%. Transfers between spouses are exempt from tax if both are domiciled in the UK.

For more information

www.naea.co.uk

The National Association of Estate Agents (NAEA) represents the interests of approximately 10,000 members who practice across all aspects of property services in the UK and overseas.

Africa

Morocco

Government
Morocco gained its independence from France in 1956 and evolved into a stable constitutional monarchy with an elected parliament. The king of Morocco has vast executive powers. It is the only African country that is not a member of the African Union; however, it is a member of the Arab League. In 2004, a revised family code that granted women more rights was pushed through parliament with the support of the king.

Society
Morocco has been subject to extensive migration and has long been the location of sedentary, urban communities that were originally settled by peoples from outside the region. Morocco is composed mainly of Berbers and Arabs. Arabic, the national and official language of Morocco, is spoken by two-thirds of the population. French and English are also used. Islam is the official state religion. The royal house, the Alawite dynasty, has ruled since the seventeenth century, basing its claim to legitimacy on descent from the Prophet Muhammad. The royal family is revered by Moroccan Muslims because of its prophetic lineage. Moroccan law mandates freedom of religion, but few non-Muslims reside in the country.

Geography

Morocco is a mountainous country in western North Africa and lies directly across the Strait of Gibraltar from Spain. The climate is Mediterranean, which becomes more extreme toward the interior regions where it is mountainous. The coastal plains are the backbone for agriculture. Forests cover about 12% of the land, and 18% of the land is arable.

Economy

Morocco has signed free trade agreements with the European Union (to take effect in 2010) and the United States. In 2006, the U.S.-Morocco Free Trade Agreement was implemented to allow no tariffs for 98% of the two-way trade of consumer and industrial products. Morocco's largest industry is the mining of phosphates. Its second-largest source of income is from nationals living abroad who transfer money to relatives living in Morocco. The third-largest source of revenue is tourism. The Moroccan government has undertaken a program of privatization and economic reform.

Types of Investments

Office buildings, commercial real estate, and second homes are the primary investments. About 120 U.S. firms now have offices, factories, subsidiaries, or joint ventures operating in Morocco. Many foreign investors are also buying real estate for personal vacation purposes and income. Morocco treats foreign and locally owned investments equally and permits 100% foreign ownership in most sectors.

Who Is Involved in Real Estate Transactions

The preliminary contract is normally drafted by an attorney. To consummate the sale, you must open a bank account in Morocco. The buyer and seller execute a final contract to convey the real estate from the buyer to the seller. At this time, the property is registered with the government, and the buyer becomes the owner of record.

Payment Methods
At the time that the initial contract is executed, the buyer deposits 30% or more of the total purchase price. In some instances, a buyer will have up to thirty days from the date that the initial contract is signed to post the deposit. The balance is due when the final agreement is executed.

Title
The buyer applies for the listing of the registered deed from the land registry in the area where the property is located. The listing must be completed within eighteen months from the date the deed was drafted. If the listing has not been applied for within the prescribed time, the applicant is fined 100% of the proportional duty payable. The land registrar can extend this deadline by six months. The registration duty is 2.5% of the property price.

Taxes and Fees
Notary tax: 0.5%
Stamp duty: 1% of property value

Buying a Single-Family Dwelling
The following lists the minimum time needed under optimum conditions and the approximate costs to complete the purchase of a dwelling after the offer has been accepted.

	Days	Cost in U.S. $
Certify signatures of the seller and buyer with notary	1	450
Obtain tax clearance certificate	38	350
Register the deed	4	2,200
Buyer applies for filing the registered deed with land registry	3	875
Total	46 days	$3,875

Debt Financing

Some mortgage lenders cater specifically to foreign investors. By using such a mortgage lender, many have found the purchase process to be relatively easy.

Inheritance

Inheritance tax is based on the property value, and the rates are dependent on the relationship of the heirs to the deceased. If you are Muslim, Moroccan law uses shariah as well as the secular family code. You are permitted to leave one-third of your property to non-family members. If you are not Muslim, you should have a will establishing who will inherit the property. If you are a nonresident, have the will notarized by the appropriate authorities.

For more information

www.moroccanamericantrade.com/business.cfm
The Moroccan American Trade and Investment Council is an American-based nonprofit trade association that promotes business in Morocco.

www.immobilierfes.com
This website lists properties available in Morocco. It is written mostly in French.

South Africa

Government

South Africa has a multiparty political system, with sixteen parties represented in parliament. The African National Congress (ANC) is the majority party in the National Assembly and controls eight of the country's nine provinces. South Africa is one of the few countries in Africa never to have had a coup d'etat, and regular elections have been held for almost a century; however, the vast majority of black South Africans were not enfranchised until 1994 when the first multiracial elections were held. The ANC won by an overwhelming majority and has been in power ever since. In 1994, the ANC adopted the Reconstruction and Development Programme as a guideline to transform South Africa from a divided society to one that provides equal opportunities for all its citizens. South Africa is one of the more socially progressive countries in Africa.

Society

As a result of immigration, South Africa is a very ethnically diverse nation, made up of people from mixed ethnic backgrounds, whites, South Asians, and blacks. Black South Africans account for slightly more than 70% of the population and represent a variety of ethnic groups. Refugees from poorer neighboring countries also make up a portion of the population. Urban blacks usually speak English or Afrikaans in addition to their native language.

The spread of AIDS is a serious problem that the government has chosen to not recognize. Many families are losing their primary wage earners, resulting in many orphans who are left to depend on the state for care and financial support. It is estimated that there are 1.1 million orphans in South Africa. Elderly people, traditionally supported by younger members of the family, are also becoming more dependent on the state for financial support.

Geography

South Africa has a long coastline that stretches more than 1,550 miles and across two oceans (the Atlantic and the Indian). It has a considerable variation in climate as well as topography. The interior is rather flat and sparsely populated. In contrast, the eastern coastline is lush and well-watered, which produces a climate similar to the tropics. The southwest has a Mediterranean climate, with wet winters and hot, dry summers. This area also produces much of South Africa's wine. On the south coast, rainfall is distributed more evenly throughout the year, producing a green landscape. This area is popularly known as the

Garden Route. South Africa has more than 20,000 different plants, which account for about 10% of the world's known species.

Economy

South Africa's economy is the largest and best developed on the continent. It has an abundant supply of resources; well-developed financial, legal, communications, energy, and transport sectors; a stock exchange that ranks among the ten largest in the world; and a modern infrastructure supporting an efficient distribution of goods to major urban centers throughout the region. However, South Africa has one of the highest rates of income inequality in the world. Most development is localized in four areas: Cape Town, Port Elizabeth, Durban, and Pretoria-Johannesburg. Beyond these economic centers, development is marginal and poverty still reigns.

Types of Investments

There are no restrictions on the types of real estate that a foreign national can invest in, and the real estate market has been profitable for foreign nationals for years. Foreign nationals own everything from office buildings to hotels and resorts. Many have purchased expensive properties as second homes or for vacation purposes. Since the end of apartheid, a greater number of people from Europe, Canada, and the United States are spending extended holidays in South Africa. Because of the high rate of foreign investment in all sectors of the economy, many foreign nationals who are living in the country for extended periods of time purchase apartments in the major urban centers. Foreign nationals are also purchasing apartments to rent to other nonresidents. House prices have risen dramatically over the past few years, by as much as 34% in some years. Although they are still rising, the rate of growth has slowed down noticeably.

Real property may be held in one of two ways: leasehold and freehold. Mineral interests as a general rule belong to the people of South Africa.

Who Is Involved in Real Estate Transactions

Real estate agents assist in selling and purchasing property and also help in managing rented properties. A notary is responsible for attesting to certain deeds, contracts, and leases. Notaries must be attorneys.

The only requirement for the sale of land is that both parties sign a sales contract and that the transfer be properly recorded. Property ownership is registered in regional deeds offices. Registration is the only legal means of obtaining title to a property, and a title deed issued by the registrar of deeds is the only valid proof of ownership. Records are accessible to the public at the various offices or online.

Title

Title may be held by individuals, partnerships, corporations, cooperative societies, and trusts.

Taxes and Fees

Agent commission: 5% to 8% of the selling price; paid by the seller

Transfer tax: 10% of the value for corporations. Individuals are assessed on a progressive scale depending on the value of the property. Exemptions are allowed in certain instances, such as purchasing unimproved land with the intent to build a residence.

Land tax: Levied by the local governments. The value of the land is determined annually.

All individuals, regardless of citizenship, and corporations who have taxable income from a source inside the country are liable for income tax. Individuals who live in the country for more than 549 days in a three-year period are taxed on their worldwide income. They are also liable for tax if living in the country for more than ninety-one days in each of the three years. Foreign residents may be able to obtain a tax credit if South Africa has a tax agreement with the taxpayer's home country.

Insurance

There is currently no title insurance.

Debt Financing

Mortgage bond rates are linked to short-term interest rates. It has recently been suggested that a fixed-rate system be introduced to reduce volatility in home loan repayments. Real property can be mortgaged as security. A full range of commercial financial institutions are available.

Inheritance

Nonresident estates are subject to an estate duty of 20% on all real property located in South Africa at the current market value. The estate is subject to capital gains tax payable by the beneficiaries.

Foreign Investment Issues

Some tribes have local autonomy, so it is important to understand the particular regulations in that area that might have an impact on the purchase of real estate. In these cases, it is recommended to have knowledgeable legal representation.

For more information

www.ieasa.org.za
The Institute of Estate Agents of South Africa is a professional body that promotes ethical standards in the industry.

www.sapoa.org.za
South African Property Owners Association is a representative body of the commercial and industrial property investment organizations.

General Resources

www.globalpropertyguide.com
This website is a good source for researching different countries. It provides information on price history, taxes, landlord-tenant laws, inheritance, and so on.

www.fiabci.com
FIABCI is an international organization that promotes the real estate profession. Its members are from sixty countries and include 100 national real estate associations representing 1.5 million professionals, including agents, lawyers, appraisers, and property managers.

www.justlanded.com
This website provides information in different languages on how to obtain visas, work permits, and find properties, as well as lists other resources for a variety of countries.

www.transparency.org
Transparency International is a politically nonpartisan organization that monitors corruption around the world in the areas of politics, public contracting, development, and the private sector.

www.icrea.org
The International Consortium of Real Estate Associations (ICREA) is a consortium of the world's leading real estate associations. It sets standards for international real estate practices and facilitates worldwide real estate transactions through its website, which has links to resources and information for a variety of countries.

www.rics.org

The Royal Institute of Chartered Surveyors promotes global standards for professionals involved in land, property, construction, and environmental issues. The website contains links to members in different countries.

www.cepi.be

Based in Belgium, this organization represents 200,000 European real estate professionals in the EU. The website provides links to property managers and property agents.

Glossary

As in any industry, there are key terms with specific meanings unique to its participants. The following list of terms is not meant to be all-inclusive. It is meant to provide the reader with basic understanding of real estate purchases and offshore terminology.

Abusive tax shelter A tax shelter that the U.S. Internal Revenue Service regards as having no economic, business, or financial purpose other than to avoid taxes.

Ad valorem taxes Taxes applicable to a property in direct relationship to the property's value.

Adjusted basis Cost of property after adjustment for certain deductions or additions as permitted or prescribed by the U.S. tax laws. In some instances, the basis of property is derived from the basis of other parties, such as a donor or an estate.

Adjusted gross income Total individual income before itemized or standard deductions and personal exemptions.

Administrator for an IRA trustee or custodian Performs duties on behalf of the custodian, which include, but are not limited to, executing applications, transfers, stock powers, escrow documents, purchase agreements, notes, deeds, reconveyances, liens, and government reporting. Often described as third-party record keepers.

Agent Person or company who acts on behalf of another person or entity as established by a contract between the parties.

Alternative investments Includes investments in private equity, real estate, oil and gas, timberlands, and distressed debt, and may include some varieties of hedge funds.

Apostille Special seal applied by an authority to certify that a document is a true copy of an original. Apostilles are available in countries that signed The Hague Convention Abolishing the Requirement of Legalization of Foreign Public Documents, popularly known as The Hague Convention. This convention, created in 1961, replaces the time-consuming chain certification process that required you to go to four different authorities to get a document certified.

Appreciated property Property with a fair market value greater than its initial cost without regard to its tax basis.

Assessed valuation Usually attributable to a taxing agency that provides a valuation of property for tax purposes. The assessed valuation may not be fair market value or an indication of comparable values.

Asset manager Person appointed by a written contract by an international business company (IBC) or an asset protection trust (APT) to direct the investment program. The account can be fully discretionary or limited. Fees to the asset manager can be based on performance, trading commissions, or a percentage of the valuation of the estate under management.

Asset protection trust (APT) Special form of an irrevocable trust, usually created offshore for the principal purpose of preserving and protecting one's wealth offshore against creditors. Title to the asset is transferred to a person named the trustee. Its ultimate function is to provide for the beneficiaries of the APT.

Assignment Method of transferring property from one individual or corporation to another. The assignment may be for any property. Endorsements on a deed or stock certificate or separate certificates may document the transfer.

Assumption An obligation taken over by the buyer of a property to be liable for payment of an existing mortgage. The buyer is substituted for the original obligor in the mortgage, and the original obligor is released from any obligation relative to the mortgage. An assumption is not a subject-to purchase (buying a property that is subject to an existing debt); however, both are used to finance the sale of property.

Badge of fraud Conduct that raises a strong presumption that it was undertaken with the intent to delay, hinder, or defraud a creditor.

Bank of International Settlements (BIS) Structured like the U.S. Federal Reserve Bank, the BIS is controlled by the Basel Committee of the G-10 nations' central banks. It sets standards for capital adequacy among the member banks.

Bank secrecy In most countries, one of the terms of the relationship between banker and customer is that the banker will keep the customer's affairs secret. Staff members are required to sign a declaration of secrecy regarding the business of the bank. Some banks use numbered accounts to limit the number of people who know the identity of the client. In certain countries, such as Switzerland and the Cayman Islands, specific legislation makes breaches of bank secrecy subject to criminal law sanctions. However, in all legal systems (including Switzerland), there are specific cases where the duty of secrecy of a banker is discharged, for example, when fraud, money laundering, and narcotics are involved. The exchange of information clause contained in most tax treaties enables the tax administration of one treaty country to obtain information concerning bank accounts that its residents have in the other treaty country.

Bank Secrecy Act Provides specific laws and rules regarding secrecy of information. Banks and their agents are required to make disclosures to clients and third parties.

Basis Cost of property for the purpose of computing gain or loss on the disposition of the property. In most cases, basis equals the purchase price.

Bearer bond Bond issued in bearer form rather than in registered form in a specific owner's name. Ownership is determined by possession.

Bearer shares Shares of stock of a corporation that are not registered in the shareholder's name. Instead, they grant ownership rights to any individual who has actual physical possession of the certificate. Bearer shares are often used to hide or disguise the ownership of the corporation. Many offshore financial secrecy jurisdictions permit the issuance of bearer shares by corporations chartered in their jurisdiction. Bearer shares may be bought, sold, or exchanged in complete privacy. They are not permitted in the United States.

Beneficial ownership True owner of an entity, asset, or transaction as opposed to any stated ownership provided in documents or oral representations. The beneficial owner is the one that receives or has the right to receive proceeds or other advantages as a result of the ownership. It is common practice in offshore financial secrecy jurisdictions to interpose entities, individuals, or both as stated owners. The beneficial or true owner is contractually acknowledged in side agreements, statements, or by other devices.

Blind pool Limited partnership where several investors pool their cash. Almost all private equity funds and the majority of private real estate funds are blind pools.

Board of trustees Board acting as a trustee of a trust or as advisors to the trustee, depending on the language of the trust indenture. See also *Committee of advisors*.

Bond In real estate, a written obligation securitized by real estate or a note.

Bridge loans Temporary financing between fundings.

Business trust Created for the primary purpose of operating or engaging in a business. A business trust is considered to be a "person" under the U.S. Internal Revenue Code. It must have a business purpose and actually function as a business.

Buy Direction Letter Letter provided to the plan administrator, trustee, or custodian that initiates the purchase of assets.

Cadastre Official register of real property, with details of the area, the owners, and the value, used in determining taxes. A cadastral map shows the boundaries and ownership details.

Cap rate For real estate investments, any rate of return used to convert income into value.

Capital Funds invested in a business that are owned by the investors of a business. Investors can be individuals, partners, or shareholders.

Captive bank Bank intended to provide services to the promoter and associates of the promoter, usually an international group of companies.

Captive insurance company Insurance company established by a company or international group to provide insurance (or reinsurance) for the promoter and the associates of the promoter.

Chain of title History of ownership of a property, its debts, liens, and other matters. In the United States, chain of title is usually evidenced by recordation made at local government agencies. In other countries, chain of title may be evidenced by entries in records of government agencies' books.

Closed-end real estate fund Private real estate fund with a fixed fund size and a limited term, typically eight to fifteen years.

Closing costs Expenses assumed by the buyer and seller to consummate a real property purchase and sale transaction. These expenses may include commissions, appraisals, surveys, title fees and title insurance, recording fees, escrow fees, attorneys' fees, documentary fees, and stamp duties. Payoffs of existing encumbrances are usually included in the closing statement.

Co-investment Investments alongside other partnerships in all types of private equity and private real estate. Co-investment allocations lower the overall cost of private equity and real estate programs.

Committee of advisors Provides nonbinding advice to the trustee and trust protector. The advisors retain an arm's-length relationship to the settlor, providing information and advice to the trustee, which may also be intended for the trustee against potential inappropriate acts.

Committee of trust protectors Alternative to using only one trust protector. Friendly toward settlor, but must remain independent.

Companies act or ordinance Legislation enacted by a tax haven to provide for the incorporation, registration, and operation of international business companies (IBCs). Commonly found in the Caribbean tax havens. For a typical example, read the Bahamas' International Business Company Act of 1989.

Controlled foreign corporation (CFC) As defined by the IRS, a foreign corporation in which over 50 percent of the stock is held by five or fewer U.S. persons who each own 10 percent or more of the stock.

Cost Amount paid for an investment for tax purposes.

Current account Used by some jurisdictions referring to an offshore personal savings or checking account.

Custodial services Service whereby a person or entity agrees to hold and manage assets on behalf of another person or entity. Not to be confused with an IRA custodian.

Custodian Bank, financial institution, or other entity that has the responsibility to manage or administer the custody or other safekeeping of assets for persons or institutions.

Debt financing Using a loan to pay for plan assets.

Deed Written document that grants title to a property to an individual or entity. The deed may transfer title from one owner to another. The grantor of title is the seller or relinquishing party who conveys the property to a grantee. The grantee is the recipient of property sold or relinquished in a transaction and is the person or entity to whom property is conveyed. Deeds generally provide an accurate description of the property conveyed. Deeds are used in the United States and many foreign countries.

Depreciation Decrease in value of a property as it is used. For IRAs, depreciation is used generally in the context of unrelated business income tax (see *Unrelated business income tax*).

Development property Investment involving substantial new construction leading to the creation of a physical asset.

Discretionary trust Grantor trust in which the trustee has complete discretion as to whom among the class of beneficiaries receives income and/or principal distributions. There are no limits on the trustee; otherwise, it would cease to be a discretionary trust. The letter of wishes could provide some guidance to the trustee without having any legal and binding effects. Provides flexibility to the trustee and the utmost privacy.

Disqualified person A person defined by the IRS who is disqualified from performing a transaction within an IRA. Common disqualified persons are spouses, lineal descendants and spouses thereof, fiduciaries and corporations, and trusts, owned by the plan participant.

Domicile Place where an individual has a permanent home or intends to return to, or in some cases, the country of origin.

Double Taxation Agreement (Double Tax Treaty) Agreement between two countries intended to relieve persons who would otherwise be subject to tax in both countries from being taxed twice.

Earnest money Funds deposited by a buyer to a seller to indicate intent to purchase a property. Generally, the conditions of the application of an earnest money deposit (sometimes referred to as a good faith deposit) are governed by the agreement of sale or purchase. The funds are usually applied to the purchase when the sale is consummated or may be used for liquidating damages.

Economic life Time period in which a property provides a return to the owner. The economic life may be profitable, and when such profitability ceases, the economic life is fully depreciated for the specific purpose it was intended to produce a profit for (see also *Depreciation*). Changes in economic life take place when the purpose of the property or investment changes, for instance because of the impact from outside forces such as government regulations and social factors.

Evasion of tax Illegal methods of tax minimization or reduction, which usually involve some element of secrecy or deception.

Exempt company A company exempted from tax or from compliance with specified regulations of the country in which it is established.

Exempt trust A trust established in a country where the government issues a guarantee that the trust income and property will not be taxed for a specified number of years, regardless of laws subsequently passed relating to income, inheritance, estate duty, or capital gains taxes.

Exequatur Recognition of a country's consul by a foreign government.

Expatriation Act or process of relinquishing citizenship or of changing one's country of permanent residence.

Fair market value Amount that would be paid by a willing seller and accepted by a willing buyer, both of whom have full knowledge of the significant facts about the property.

Family holding trust Created specifically to hold a family's assets consisting of real and/or personal property.

Family limited partnership (FLP) Partnership owned entirely by members of the same family. Created for family estate planning and some asset protection. A highly appreciated asset is transferred into the FLP to achieve a capital gains tax reduction. Usually, the parents are the general partners holding a 1–2 percent interest. The other family members are the limited partners holding the balance of the interest.

Fee simple Unrestricted ownership of property by an individual.

Fictitious invoice It is common practice in the offshore industry to issue false invoices as a means to transfer money to an offshore jurisdiction to achieve a tax deduction for the paying entity. Commonly, an entity associated with an offshore promoter issues the invoice.

Financial secrecy Confidentiality afforded to financial transactions either by enactment of law or by other means. There are many forms of financial secrecy. It can be part of an agreement between an institution and a client. Law can impose it with either criminal or civil sanctions. A financial institution can operationally give financial secrecy by allowing only top management to know who owns an account or using numbered accounts.

Flight capital Money that flows offshore and likely never returns. Flight is exacerbated by a lack of confidence as government grows without bounds.

Foreign bank accounts Every U.S. resident, partnership, corporation, estate, or trust must advise the U.S. Treasury of any financial interest in or signature authority over a foreign bank, securities, or other financial account in a foreign country and must report that relationship each calendar year by filing Form 90-22.1 with the Treasury Department on or before June 30 of the succeeding year. A foreign country includes all geographical areas located outside the United States, Guam, Puerto Rico, and the U.S. Virgin Islands.

Foreign corporation A corporation domiciled in a different country. Within the United States, a foreign corporation can also be a corporation in another state.

Foreign grantor trust A trust that is located and administered outside the United States. The U.S. person who funds the trust is generally treated as the owner of the assets of the trust for tax purposes. A foreign trust is one in which any decisions of the trustee are not subject to the jurisdiction of a U.S. court.

Foreign Investor in Real Property Tax Act of 1980 (FIRPTA) Under FIRPTA and the Economic Recovery Act of 1981, unless an exemption is granted by the IRS, upon the sale of real property owned by offshore (foreign) persons, the agency, attorney, or escrow officer handling the transaction is required to withhold capital gains taxes at the closing of the sale transaction. Unless withheld and submitted to the IRS, the party handling the sale transaction is personally liable for the taxes.

Foreign person Any person, including a U.S. citizen, who resides outside the United States or is subject to the jurisdiction and laws of a country other than the United States.

Foreign personal holding company A foreign corporation in which more than 50 percent of the total combined voting power of all classes of voting stock or the total value of the stock is owned by or for no more than five U.S. persons.

Foreign sales corporation Special category of a foreign corporation owned by U.S. persons that was given U.S. tax incentives for export sales. This tax provision was repealed by the FSC Repeal and Extraterritorial Income Exclusion Act of 2000, which also provided tax incentives for exporting.

Foreign source income Income derived from sources outside the United States, such as employment in a foreign country, income from a business or real estate located within a foreign country, dividends from foreign corporations, and other investment income from foreign sources.

Foreign tax credit Credit toward U.S. income taxes for the amount of income taxes paid to a foreign country on the same income.

Fraudulent conveyance Transfer of an asset that violates the fraudulent conveyance statutes of the affected jurisdictions.

Free port and free zone Designated areas that receive special treatment through their exclusion from the country's normal customs rules. A free port is one at which imports may be landed without paying customs duties. Though free zones are often part of a tax incentive package in what would otherwise be a high-tax jurisdiction, they may also be found in tax havens, such as Freeport in the Bahamas.

Good faith deposit See *Earnest money*.

Grantor Person who creates and funds a trust for the benefit of another, where the person who funds the trust is treated as the owner of the trust assets.

Headquarters company A company organized in a foreign country, usually a tax haven, and that exclusively services its affiliate companies through managing or administering activities. It does not buy or sell products and does not involve itself in financing activities as may be practiced by offshore holding companies. A headquarters company is a fixed installation belonging to a foreign enterprise or an international company having its registered office in a specific foreign country selected because its laws permit it to act for the sole benefit of one or more companies in a group for the purpose of performing management control, servicing, or coordination functions, usually in a specified geographical area. The headquarters company generally is allowed a tax deduction by granting permission to base its taxation on a national profit amounting to approximately 5–8 percent of the total operating expenses incurred in the particular country where it is organized. In some countries, there is no taxation on income, and expenses are not used as any base of computation. In other countries, the headquarters company may be either an incorporated company of the host country or a branch of an international company.

Holding company A company whose activity is limited to holding and managing investments or property but not having ordinary commercial or trading activities. The requirements to achieve holding company status vary in different countries (in particular, Liechtenstein, Luxembourg, Nauru, and the Netherlands).

Inbound Coming into the United States, such as funds being paid to a U.S. person from an offshore entity.

Indirect investments Investments held by an intermediate legal entity such as a corporation or trust, rather than in the name of the individual taxpayer.

INTERFIPOL International Fiscal Police. The tax crime counterpart to Interpol (see *Interpol*).

Internal rate of return (IRR) Standard return calculation methodology in private equity and real estate. It is the discount rate that equates the net present value (NPV) of an investment's cash inflows with its cash outflows, or the annual effective compounded rate of return.

International business company or international business corporation (IBC) A corporation formed in an offshore financial secrecy jurisdiction that is afforded certain tax advantages and protection as to the disclosure of its beneficial owner. Depending on the offshore financial secrecy jurisdiction, shareholders of the IBC may remain confidential through the use of bearer shares (see *Bearer shares*). Just as with U.S. corporations, the same person may act as a shareholder, director, president, agent, or as any other officer within the company. Generally, however, the beneficial owners appoint resident officers and directors. Typically, an IBC is authorized to do business anywhere in the world, except in its home country where it was incorporated. The IBC may purchase real estate, cars, businesses, and so forth. The beneficial owner may act as an agent of the IBC to purchase assets on its behalf. Assets are held under a corporate name, thereby helping to protect the beneficial owner's privacy. It has been reported that there are over 1 million IBCs formed in offshore jurisdictions worldwide.

International financial centre (IFC) A country identified as a tax haven.

International trust A Cook Islands term for a special type of an APT (see *Asset protection trust*). Governed by the laws of the Cook Islands.

Interpol International Criminal Police Organization. A network of multinational law enforcement authorities established to exchange information regarding money laundering and other criminal activities. It includes more than 125 member nations.

Inversion Transaction through which the corporate structure of a U.S.-based multinational group is altered so that a new foreign corporation, typically located in a low- or no-tax country, replaces the existing U.S. parent corporation as the parent of the corporate group.

Layered trusts Trusts placed in series where the beneficiary of the first trust is the second trust. Layered trusts are used for privacy. Layering is achieved with numerous combinations of entities, for example, 100 percent of the shares of an IBC owned by the first trust, which has as its sole beneficiary a second trust (see *International business company or international business corporation*).

Letter box company Corporation set up in a tax haven with nothing more than a mailing address to take advantage of tax provisions. Severely criticized in many quarters as an evasive measure, the establishment of companies with little more than a nameplate has been outlawed in Monaco, but it is allowed to function in many other tax havens.

Letter of wishes Document that purportedly has no legal status. The document transmits the wishes of the creator or the alleged owner of the trust to the trustee. A letter of wishes is not a part of the trust instrument. It is generally used by the beneficial owner of the trust assets to retain some control over the trust assets. Trustees normally welcome this tool, because it enables them to exercise their discretion while having the wishes of the grantor in mind. The trustee may consider the letter but is not bound or otherwise accountable by its terms. In reality, the letter of wishes is honored as if it were a binding legal document. Although a letter of wishes is frequently associated with abusive trusts, both domestic and offshore, it is also used as a part of normal estate planning and in other contexts for legitimate purposes. Sometimes referred to as a side letter.

Leveraged transaction Using borrowed funds for part of a purchase. Also known as debt financing.

Limited company Not an international business company. May be a resident of the tax haven and is set up under a special company act with a simpler body of administrative laws.

Limited liability company (LLC) A legal entity that protects the members from personal liability arising from damages caused by the company or its employees. Similar to a corporation that is taxed as a partnership or as an S-corporation. Consists of member owners and a manager, at a minimum. This form of company also helps to protect the assets owned by the LLC from creditors' claims on the members of the LLC. An LLC combines the more favorable characteristics of a corporation and a partnership. It permits the complete pass-through of tax advantages and operational flexibility found in a partnership, operating in a corporate-style structure, with limited liability.

Limited liability limited partnership (LLLP) Protects the general partners from liability. Previously, the general partner was a corporation to protect the principals from personal liability. Under an LLLP, an individual can be a general partner and have limited personal liability.

Limited liability partnership Form of an LLC that is favored by professional associations, such as accountants and attorneys (see *Limited liability company*).

Limited partnership A partnership composed of one or more general partners who manage the partnership, and limited partners who have no personal liability for debts of the limited partnership beyond the amounts invested. General partners are liable for any debts of the partnership in excess of the partnership assets.

Loan-to-value ratio Ratio of the current level of financing for a property investment to the fair market value for that investment. This is a considered factor when obtaining debt financing.

Mutual Legal Assistance Treaty (MLAT) Agreement among the United States and many Caribbean countries for the exchange of information for the enforcement of criminal laws. U.S. tax evasion is excluded as a crime to the offshore countries. The British Virgin Islands have not executed the MLAT.

Nominee Individual or entity that acts on behalf of a beneficial owner. Most often the nominee pretends to be the owner of an entity, asset, or transaction to provide a veil of secrecy regarding the beneficial owner's involvement. Many offshore entities provide a nominee to act as owner of the arrangement, but generally the nominee will not act unless instructed to by the beneficial owner.

Nominee director Someone who acts as a "front" director of a company. In some jurisdictions, the nominee director can also be another offshore company. Every IBC must have a board of directors, which may consist of one person or many. For instance, the beneficial owner can appoint oneself as the director and sole officer of the corporation. However, most IBCs are formed with a nominee director. The nominee may be, but does not have to be, an individual who works and/or resides in the country where the IBC was formed. The nominee may be used to sign documents, such as contracts or loans, if the beneficial owner does not want his or her signature connected with the corporation. Typically, the nominee director has no knowledge of the IBC's affairs or accounts, cannot control or influence the IBC, and does not act unless instructed to by the beneficial owner (see *International business company or international business corporation*).

Nongrantor trust Usually an APT (see *Asset protection trust*) created by a nonresident alien on behalf of the U.S. beneficiaries.

Nonresident alien Person or entity that is not a citizen or permanent resident.

Nonresident company Company treated by the jurisdiction in which it is incorporated as nonresident for tax purposes, exchange control purposes, or both.

Notary Civil law notaries, as opposed to notaries public, are trained jurists or solicitors who are usually limited to areas of private law, such as real estate–related activities. The types of tasks the notary performs regarding real estate transactions varies from country to country. For example, in France the notaire performs complete legal services in the acquisition and disposition of property. In many Spanish-speaking countries, the duties of the *notario* may range from officially acknowledging document signatures, much like a notary public, to comprehensive legal services.

Obligor Person or company that is obligated to make payments. Also known as the transferee or buyer.

Offshore International term meaning not only out of your country (jurisdiction) but also out of the tax reach of your country of residence or citizenship. Synonymous with "foreign," "transnational," "global," "international," "transworld," and "multinational." The IRS tends to use "foreign." When referring to a country, it means a jurisdiction that offers financial secrecy laws to attract investment from outside its borders. When referring to a financial institution, it means that the institution primarily offers services to persons domiciled outside the jurisdiction of the country in which the financial institution is organized.

Offshore banking Usually refers to the establishment and operation of U.S. or foreign banks in offshore tax havens such as the Bahamas and Cayman Islands.

Offshore banking unit (OBU) Bank in an offshore financial center. The bank is not allowed to conduct business in the domestic market. It can only conduct business with other OBUs or with foreign persons.

Offshore finance company (OFC) A company organized in a foreign country, almost always in a tax-haven country, that handles such financing services as arranging foreign loans in euro-currency markets, floating bonds, and financing other forms of indebtedness in U.S. dollars or other hard currencies. Generally, the OFC is created to handle the financing requirements of its parent or related companies, but is used occasionally to handle the financing needs of the parent company's distributors or agents overseas.

Offshore fund Mutual fund offering its shares to persons resident outside the country in which it is incorporated.

Offshore Group of Banking Supervisors (OGBS) Established in 1980 at the instigation of the Basel Committee on Banking Supervision, with which the OGBS maintains close contact. Its primary objective is to promote the effective supervision of banks in their jurisdictions and to further international cooperation between member nations and other banking supervisors.

Offshore holding company A company organized in a foreign country that controls one or more affiliate companies and manages, administers, or services its affiliate companies usually located outside the country in which the parent company is incorporated.

Offshore investment center A financial center used as a foreign base for overseas operations where the investor may move in and out of the investment freely. Large amounts of financial assets or foreign currencies may be sold without delay at low cost as compared with other types of financial centers. An offshore investment center is also used as a base for international activities such as export-import trading, commodity transactions, mutual and other investment funds, exchange and securities hedging, futures trading for options, calls and puts, and patent and trademark licensing.

Offshore mail forwarding address Often an IBC's offshore address is nothing more than a mail drop (post office box). Bank and brokerage statements and any other type of company mail is sent to this address. The mail is typically picked up twice monthly by an offshore facilitator and put into a plain, brown envelope and mailed to the address of the beneficial owner's choice. Only the domestic return address and the recipient's address appear on the envelope. Using offshore mail forwarding ensures that the wrong eyes never view sensitive offshore mail.

Offshore profit center Branch of a major international bank or multinational corporation that is established in a low-tax financial jurisdiction to lower taxes for the business entity as a whole. The resulting taxed profits are blended to enhance the overall return to the shareholders.

Offshore promoter Person or entity who markets offshore arrangements to the public. The promoter can be a financial institution, a lawyer, an accountant, a broker, a financial planner, or another individual.

Open-end real estate fund Fund with a long-term life during which new investors can be admitted on an ongoing basis and existing investors can make contributions or withdrawals at their discretion. Open-end funds typically reinvest all operating and capital cash flows, unless required to meet withdrawal requests.

Personal investment corporation (PIC) Term used in the banking industry to refer to an IBC. PICs are generally created for the private bank's client to hold investment assets (see *International business company or international business corporation*).

Prefiling notice Mailed by the IRS to taxpayers who are believed to be participating in fraudulent trust programs. The notice requests that the receiver seek professional counsel before filing the next tax return.

Private banking Offshore banking services are most commonly handled by the private banking departments of commercial banks or by private banks that cater solely to private banking clientele. "Private banking" is a relatively recent term that refers to a higher level of financial services afforded to a bank's wealthiest clients, functioning as a bank within a bank, it maintains its own separate books and records and is subject to separate operating procedures. Private banking activities are conducted through relationship managers and marketing officers who have access to a team of specialists around the world to provide personal money management, financial advice, and investment services. Private bankers are in a unique position of having knowledge and understanding of their client's personal and business backgrounds, sources of wealth, and uses of private banking accounts. Private banking is not usually associated with abusive tax schemes.

Prohibited transaction Any improper use of an IRA or plan by the plan participant or any disqualified person.

Ready-made company See *Shelf company.*

Real estate investment trust (REIT) An investment trust that invests in real estate properties and/or in debt obligations secured by real estate. A REIT permits a large number of investors to passively participate in the investment or purchase of real estate. A REIT must be composed of at least 100 members. Real estate in a REIT is not owned by the individual investors. The shares are freely transferable and are treated as partnership interests instead of corporations for tax purposes.

Red Cross scheme A scheme that uses a charitable entity to disguise a transfer of funds offshore. For example, $1 million is donated to a charitable organization. The charitable organization then remits a portion of the "donation" to an account offshore and retains a portion of the initial donation.

Registered company A company that is registered with the authorities of the country in which it is established. In most countries, it is illegal to operate as a company without being registered.

Resident alien In the United States, a person who lives in the country for an extended period but who is not a citizen of the United States. Resident aliens are subject to U.S. tax laws.

Revenue Reconciliation Act of 1995 Proposed changes to the U.S. Internal Revenue Code affecting foreign trust reporting, among other changes.

Sales agreement A contract in which a seller agrees to sell and a buyer agrees to buy property subject to the written terms and conditions. Also known as a contract of sale, contract for purchase, or residential or commercial sales agreement.

Self-direction When used in context of IRAs and qualified plans, it is the ability of the account holder or plan participant to direct how the assets are invested. The extent to which self-direction is permitted is governed by the IRS form 5305 IRA agreement and the plan and trust document for qualified plans. IRA custodians or trustees may limit the extent to which an account holder may self-direct by including and excluding plan options in Form 5305. Plan trustees may make the same limitations in the plan and trust documentation.

Settle To create or establish an offshore trust. Done by the settlor (offshore term) or the grantor (U.S. and IRS term).

Settlor Person who creates and provides the funds for a trust.

Shelf company When a company that has been organized with designated capital and has paid the registration costs is placed on an inactive basis. The annual registration and the capital and stamp duty fees are currently paid, but shares are held in bearer form. The directors and officers are substituted at the time the company is taken off the shelf and becomes active.

Société Anonyme A limited liability corporation established under French law. Requires a minimum of seven shareholders. In Spanish-speaking countries, it is known as the Sociedad Anonima. Important characteristic of both is that the liability of the shareholders is limited up to the amount of their capital contribution.

Stamp duty Form of tax that is levied on documents. Typically, a physical stamp must be attached to or impressed upon the document to denote that the stamp duty has been paid before the document becomes legally effective. Some countries have a stamp duty levied on real estate transactions.

Suffixes Name or abbreviation of letters after a company name to denote limited liability. Some examples are: Limited, Corporation, Incorporated, Société Anonyme (France), Société par actions (France), Sociedad Anonima, Sociedade Anonima, Stiftung (Liechtenstein), Limitada, Aktiengesellschaft (Germany), Naamloze Vennootschap (Netherlands), Aktieselskab (Denmark), Sociedad Berhad Anonima

(Western Samoa), Berhad (Lebanon), Sociedad Anónima de Inversión (Uruguay), AG (Germany), ApS, A/S (Denmark), BV (Netherlands), Corp., Est. (Liechtenstein), GmbH (Germany), Inc., KFT (Hungary), LDA, LLC, Ltd., PLC (United Kingdom), RT (Hungary), S.A., S.A.R.L. (France), S.A.F.I. (Uruguay).

Tax avoidance Legal methods of tax minimization or reduction.

Tax clearance certificate Issued by an income tax department confirming that an individual departing from a country has fulfilled all income tax obligations and has no arrears. The certificate must be shown to customs and emigration authorities upon departure.

Tax evasion Fraudulent or illegal arrangements made with the intention of evading tax, for example, failing to make full disclosure to the revenue authorities.

Tax-exempt company A company designed for companies and individuals who are foreign to the jurisdiction in which it is registered, providing a maximum of privacy combined with comprehensive freedoms from local taxation. A tax-exempt company (often referred to as an exempt company) pays a fixed annual fee to exempt the company from further tax liabilities in the jurisdiction in which it is registered. It also has to pay annual filing fees (governmental fees) and domiciliary fees (service provider's fees) to remain registered.

Tax haven A country that provides a no-tax or low-tax environment. The United States is considered a tax haven by some countries. In some offshore jurisdictions, a regimen of reduced tax is aimed toward entities organized in the country that have all operations occurring outside the country. These countries seek to encourage investment and make up revenue losses by charging a variety of start-up and annual fees.

Tax regimen Local tax treatment of income tax, foreign source income, nonresident treatment, and special tax concessions that, when combined, form complex issues.

Tax shelter An investment or financial transaction that is designed to generate substantial tax deductions or credits.

Tax treaties International agreements or conventions with the object of eliminating double taxation by the contracting countries. International double taxation is loosely defined as the imposition of comparable taxes in two (or more) countries on the same taxpayer in respect of the same subject matter and for identical or overlapping periods. The most harmful effects of double taxation are on the exchange of goods and services and on the movement of capital and persons.

Tax withholding Withholding and other taxes are frequently imposed on rental income received from real estate in a foreign country. Similarly, capital gains tax may be imposed on the profit made from the sale of property. However, in exceptional cases, the provisions of a tax treaty, for example, the treaty between the Netherlands Antilles and the United States, may minimize the total tax burden. Ownership of real estate by individuals may also result in liability to death duties and similar taxes in the country in which the real estate is situated, regardless of the individual owner's residence or domicile. For this reason, it is common to hold foreign real estate through a tax haven or other company.

Third-party record keepers for an IRA trustee or custodian Bank and trust companies may appoint one or more record keepers for IRAs. The record keeper performs duties on behalf of the custodian, which include but are not limited to executing applications, transfers, stock powers, escrow documents, purchase agreements, notes, deeds, reconveyances, liens, and government reporting for depositors.

Tranch A bond series issued for sale in a foreign country.

Trust An entity created for the purpose of protecting and conserving assets for the benefit of a third party, the beneficiary. A contract affecting three parties: the settlor, the trustee, and the beneficiary.

A trust protector is optional but recommended as well. In the trust, the settlor transfers asset ownership to the trustee on behalf of the beneficiaries.

Trust deed An asset protection trust document or instrument.

Trust indenture A trust instrument, such as a trust deed creating an offshore trust.

Trust protector A person appointed by the settlor to oversee the trust on behalf of the beneficiaries. In many jurisdictions, local trust laws define the concept of the trust protector. The trust protector has veto power over the trustee with respect to discretionary matters but no say with respect to issues unequivocally covered in the trust deed. Trust decisions are the trustee's alone. The trust protector has the power to remove the trustee and appoint trustees. The protector consults with the settlor, but the final decisions must be the protector's.

Trustee A person totally independent of the settlor who has the fiduciary responsibility to the beneficiaries to manage the trust and or the assets of the trust as a reasonable prudent business person would do in the same circumstances. Where applicable, defers to the trust protector when required in the best interest of the trust. The trustee reporting requirements are defined at the onset and should include how often, to whom, and how to respond to instructions or inquiries, global investment strategies, fees (flat and/or percentage of the valuation of the trust estate), anticipated future increases in fees, hourly rates for consulting services, seminars and client educational materials, and so forth. The trustee may have full discretionary powers of distributions to beneficiaries. In the case of an Individual Retirement Arrangement, a passive trustee who has no investment decision-making capability for a self-directed plan is not a fiduciary to the plan assets.

Unimproved property Related to land that is vacant and has no improvements that would make the property serve a useful purpose.

Unrelated business income tax (UBIT) A tax imposed by the IRS that applies to any profit made on operating income of certain tax-favored entities in excess of $1,000.

Unrelated debt-financed income tax A tax imposed by the IRS that applies to any profit made on debt-financed income of certain tax-favored entities in excess of $1,000.

U.S. person A U.S. person is a citizen, a resident alien individual, a domestic trust, estate, partnership, or corporation of the United States.

U.S. source income Income derived from sources in the United States, such as from employment in the United States, income from a U.S.-based trade or business, and most types of investment income from U.S. real estate, corporate dividends, and interest on debt issued by U.S. persons.

Value-added real estate fund Marketing term used to describe a broad range of real estate funds that engage in active strategies to create value in their underlying property investments. Such funds target a broad range of returns and typically use modest to high levels of leverage.

Value-added tax (VAT) Taxation based on the sale price of various goods or services. The amount of tax paid by the supplier is deducted from the total due by the seller.

Vintage company See *Shelf company*.

Worldwide taxation The United States imposes income, estate, and gift taxes on the worldwide income and assets of its citizens and permanent residents, regardless of where the income is earned, where the assets are located, or where the citizen or resident is living at the time.

Index

About the Author

Hubert Franz-Josef Bromma, a native of Austria, has been active in financial industries since 1967. He has been involved with real estate, qualified plans (Keoghs), and IRAs since then. He was the general partner of Associated Administrators, Ltd., an IRA and Keogh administration firm founded in 1969, prior to becoming the CEO of Providence Trust Company, where he remained until 1992. He also developed the first truly self-directed IRA for a number of banks in 1981. His highly successful bank and S&L consulting firm, Consulting Associates, performed fifty mergers, divestitures, and acquisitions during the 1980s. He is currently the CEO of Entrust Administration, Inc., a firm that has acted as agent for custodian banks throughout the United States since 1981.

Bromma has written numerous articles and several books over the last twenty years and speaks regularly to pension, investment, and real estate groups throughout the world. He completed his advanced degrees in policy administration, economics, and political science in a combined program from San Francisco State University and the University of California, Berkeley.

He has also been on the San Francisco Blue Ribbon Committee on Management and a special consultant to the Municipal Court of that city. He currently is an active lecturer for charitable organizations, as well as colleges and universities. Bromma is also on the board of directors for several small- and medium-sized businesses and philanthropic organizations.

ELF-DIRECTED RETIREMENT PLAN SERVICES | SELF-DIRECTED RETIREMENT PLAN SERVICES | SELF-DIRECTE

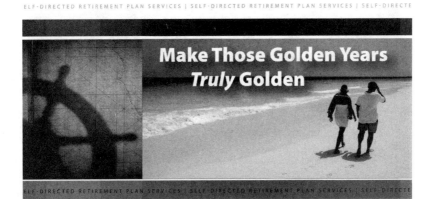

Make Those Golden Years *Truly* **Golden**

ELF-DIRECTED RETIREMENT PLAN SERVICES | SELF-DIRECTED RETIREMENT PLAN SERVICES | SELF-DIRECTE

A World of Offshore Investment Opportunities

- Real Property
- Currency
- LLCs
- Stocks
- Mutual Funds

Discover the benefits of investing offshore with your IRA or 404(k)

Why limit yourself to traditional investments when there's a world of opportunity out there? A self-directed retirement account gives you the freedom to invest in currency, limited partnerships and many other offshore assets.

For over 25 years, Entrust has helped our clients understand the broad spectrum of retirement investments permitted by the IRS. Entrust's nationwide network of professionals have first-hand knowledge about managing self-directed investments in the U.S. and offshore. Benefit from their expertise and open a self-directed retirement account today.

Call (888) 340-8977, or visit *www.TheEntrustGroup.com*.

Get started today!

En**trust Group**
The

Self-Directed Retirement Plan Services

Nationwide Network of Offices

(888) 340-8977

SAVE BIG ON TAXES & CREATE TRUE REAL ESTATE WEALTH WITH HUGH BROMMA

"Hugh Bromma is THE EXPERT on tax free and tax deferred investing. This book is worth ten times its weight in gold."

— Jim Hogan, President, Hogan School of Real Estate, Inc

Get out of the slow-growing mutual fund investment rut and buy and sell your way to real estate wealth with the funds in your retirement account.

Bromma helps you maximize profits and minimize taxes on every overseas investment opportunity, no matter how far away.

Learn more. Do more.

AVAILABLE EVERYWHERE BOOKS ARE SOLD